To

Keep

and never

goal. Grace and

Joe

goal. Sept 2017

The Ghost of Perfection

The Ghost of Perfection

Searching for Humanity

JOSEPH HAWARD

Foreword by Michael Hardin

RESOURCE *Publications* · Eugene, Oregon

Resource Publications
An Imprint of Wipf and Stock Publishers
199 W. 8th Ave., Suite 3
Eugene, OR 97401

www.wipfandstock.com

PAPERBACK ISBN: 978-1-5326-1489-7
HARDCOVER ISBN: 978-1-5326-1491-0
EBOOK ISBN: 978-1-5326-1490-3

Manufactured in the U.S.A.   MAY 23, 2017

For Sarah, Grace and Lizzie. My world.

Contents

Foreword

In the United States we are less than 100 days into a political and social experiment that has polarized Christians and churches in America. On the one hand is a white middle class to upper class segment of the population, a small minority who subscribe in one form or another to a theology of dominion and actually preach, teach and catechize about the greatness of the USA, the importance of good citizenship, which is nothing more than equivalence to a certain moral code, and worse still is that this theological model valorizes war, torture and human suffering. The patriotic elements of this message are a staple of impoverished churches.

There may well come a time of much more significant crisis to American Christianity in the coming years. It may be that the proclamation of the Gospel will be shut down by the political hegemony this theological minority control. We may end up having to call a 'Confessing Church' into being. Much remains to happen before that can happen of course, but it is not difficult to suggest such a course for the future. The Age of Anger in which we live is well described by Pinkaj Mishna and its apocalyptic overtones echo those of Girard, Žižek, Ellul as well as numerous futurists and climatologists. The world as we know is changing, morphing into something else.

In addition, over the past three score years theology and biblical studies have gone through major changes with entire hypotheses and theories being abandoned and new paradigms tried on one after another in the academy like someone tries on shirts in a department store dressing room. One could, and many have, become distressed about the plethora of research that has been done, the hundreds of thousands of books and dissertations written, and the many, varied and competing theories that clamor for attention. Little wonder that it seems that most of contemporary American Christendom is floating on an ocean with a major storm brewing.

Christendom seems for the most part to be in survival mode with its apologetics, its tainted glory, and its defensive moral, social and political maneuvers. The churches self-justification for existence, its view of a punishing god, a god embedded in economies of exchange, a god who tortures, commits genocide, justifies war and violence; all contribute to the dying of Protestantism. This kind of a god just is not worth knowing and no amount of fear can make anybody love such a deity. The days of hellfire and brimstone preaching, the days of announcing a wrathful god as 'good news' (sic) are finally going the way of the dinosaur.

Which brings me to this book you have in your hand. One of the pleasures of finally having some grey hair is that one meets younger women and men whose passion for Jesus and for the Gospel knows no limits. Nothing stops such young adults from questioning everything and reading everything they can get their hands on. Joe Haward is one such preacher for whom I not only have deep respect but also much affection. He is a British Baptist pastor and I daresay the UK Baptist Union would do well to heed his clarion call in *The Ghost of Perfection* for it is the Gospel, pure, undefiled, intelligent, witty and full of transformative power.

The Ghost of Perfection is a multi-perspective analysis of the major symptoms of the disease plaguing Protestant Christianity, viz., a sacrificial hermeneutic. If in times past one identified the marks of Christianity as "one, holy, catholic and apostolic" today Joe Haward has put his finger on the marks of contemporary Christendom with the brazen fearlessness of a Hebrew Prophet like Amos. These marks of triumphalism testify to a Christianity apart from the Cross of Christ, a Christianity living in a faux realized eschatology replete with big houses, luxury cars, hefty bank accounts, swimming pools, country club memberships and elegant soirees. This Christianity is touted on Christian television, radio, and from publishing houses, most religious best sellers have to do with improving one's life or wallet. This is a Christianity that is haunted by the ghost of perfection. So how do we escape such a vicious box?

If we are going to reframe our theology we must first rethink our anthropology; we humans have a tendency to make God from our own image. One way to do this is to engage the discipline of theological anthropology. This is what *The Ghost of Perfection* really is: a theological anthropology richly sourced from cinema, novels, philosophers, biblical scholars, philosophers and others. This pastoral inter-disciplinary style is what makes this a fascinating read; the content, the solutions Pastor Haward offers make this book indispensable. I wish someone had written a book like this thirty years ago when I was a pastor. It is a pleasure and a delight to commend this Joseph Haward and his debut work *The Ghost of Perfection*.

Michael Hardin
Executive Director, Preaching Peace
Lancaster PA
Holy Week 2017

Preface

The Ghost of Perfection evolved from the world around me. In many ways it is an expression of my inner self, seeking to understand some of the challenges I see all around, a book that is trying to make sense of much that, at times, makes little sense. When I became a follower of Jesus at the age of twenty-one, faith was very clear to me, the answers readily available. I spoke to people with a certainty of who God is, and the need to be saved from the world around them. Then life enters the stage of faith, dancing a different song to the one you were sure existed, and the answers do not come so readily, the certainty fades with the lives of real people, their suffering, their joy, their beauty and brokenness; their humanity. So I began to read. Of course I had read before, but after finishing my theology degree I had been introduced to ancient and modern people who had said many things about all the questions that were circulating through me. I read the early church fathers, atheists, philosophers, theologians, novelists, and mystics. I started to write a blog, journal, and use social media to express the questions that were coursing within. Yet I knew I had to express the questions and thoughts more concretely and bring them together with greater clarity. It was out of this wrestling that I decided to write a book.

Reading the Gospels, the New Testament, and theology, I began to see that God was in the business of making people more human, and anything that mars, damages, or even destroys that humanity is to be sharply critiqued, confronted, challenged, and fought against. It seems to me that this is what Jesus did, and this is what Jesus continues to do through his Spirit. *The Ghost of Perfection* is the beginning of my evolving thoughts around what it means to be human in light of the person of Jesus, and the challenges to our humanity faced by western culture and religion, particularly Western Christianity. I believe there are legitimate questions that need to be asked of the Western church in regard to theology and the resulting practice that this theology produces. A friend who read the first draft suggested my critique was so severely stinging that I lost the message of hope that I was seeking to convey. I trust that what you have before you is a more balanced and hopeful version, and yet does not make light of the genuine damage poor theology does to people within our communities.

As a thirty-something year old I am a millennial apparently, and as a result, the way I view the world is shaped by a rapidly changing landscape in a time of increased technological advancement. I would argue that social media, the way the internet functions today, consumerism, and identity have given rise to complexities and huge challenges regarding our humanity. And yet, when reading ancient and modern writers, we see themes surrounding sex and violence and identity that have been with us since the dawn of our existence. *The Ghost of Perfection* is my small attempt to bring together some of the great thinkers, to examine some of these recurring themes, and to offer a picture of humanity that brings us to our senses. Or, to put it another way, in the human being, Jesus of Nazareth, we encounter humanity as we should be, and in that humanity we discover our true selves. Someone wondered whether my use of modern fiction in films, books, and television to highlight certain points throughout the book would actually hinder the message and make it irrelevant in such a fast-paced society where yesterday's news is quickly forgotten. I think this is a valid point, yet my hope is that the *way* I use works of fiction will enable the light of truthfulness to shine upon our culture, whatever age we live in. Indeed, my desire is that as people read the book and hear the suggestions I make, they will be able to look at their own world, the books they read, the films they watch, the news they receive, and have their spiritual and intellectual eyes opened to the points I am seeking to make within these pages. I have tried to write in such a way that those who have little theological background will find it accessible yet also challenging, a challenge they want to pursue beyond this book, and those who are well versed in theology will hear the deeper threads running through and be able to develop them beyond this book.

It was my wife Sarah who came up with the title one evening as we sat watching the UK's Channel 4 property program *Location, Location, Location*. In this particular episode, and common to many of the episodes, a couple had within their minds a house they wanted to buy, and yet every house they looked at did not match up to their desire or expectation. "The ghost of perfection," Sarah remarked. It was a throw-away comment, but it was brilliant, and it got to the heart of this book I was working on. Today Sarah cannot remember saying it, such was its spontaneity, and this, interestingly enough, is the point too: we are a spontaneous, fleeting, changing culture, moving on to the next thing, searching for something, but never entirely sure what it is we are looking for, and then forgetting how we even got to where we find ourselves. My hope is that this book will either help you stop and say, "Ah, yes!" and begin a conversation within you and then with others as to what it means to be human, or will help you bring clarity to thoughts and ideas that you have been already wrestling with. More than that, though, my hope is that through these pages you will be able to name that which strips, and breaks, mars, and destroys your humanity, and, more positively, celebrate, pursue, and reclaim the humanity you are beckoned towards.

My thanks to Wipf and Stock for their support and desire to see this work find the light of day. They are a publisher who are willing to take a risk. Thank you to Peter Bell who worked so hard on this to make it far better than I could ever have made it. To Michael Hardin for his continued support, help, wisdom, and theological depth, thank you. Many of us would testify to your influence and positivity in our lives; some have called it "taking the red pill"! To all those that read the first draft and helpfully critiqued it: John Colwell, Jeff Jacobson, Dan Foster; thank you, friends. To my family for making sure I never let my ideas lose sight of reality; Mum, Dad, Cas, Mary, and Bram. To my identical twin Tom for simply being who he is; thank you for inspiring me with your own story. And thank you to my three beautiful girls: my wife Sarah and two daughters, Grace and Lizzie. Your patience, kindness, and unconditional love transform me daily, show me Jesus, and lead me beyond ghostly versions of myself, enabling me to be more human. This book is dedicated to you. I love you

Revd Joseph Haward
This Hope
Newton Abbot, UK
2017

Abbreviations

Throughout this book the following abbreviation is used:

ANF   Ante-Nicene Father of the Christian Church, 10 vols., eds. Alexander Roberts and James Donaldson (Edinburgh: T & T Clark/Grand Rapids, MI: Eerdmans, 1993–97 [1885–96]).

Introduction

Dreamers

What is the most resilient parasite? Bacteria? A virus? An intestinal worm?
An idea.
Resilient, highly contagious. Once an idea has taken hold of the brain, it's almost
impossible to eradicate. An idea that is fully formed—fully understood—that
sticks, right in there somewhere.

COBB, *INCEPTION*

What does it mean to be human? With the ancients, have we not each
looked to the heavens and asked,

> What are human beings that you are mindful of them,
>   mortals that you care for them? (Ps 8:4)

This, then, is a book about what it means to be human. Through these pages
I will seek to ask the question, "What are human beings?" and in doing so
challenge some of those ways our humanity is stripped from us. More than
that, though, we will discover together what it positively means to be human
and how we might pursue, reclaim, and celebrate our humanness, a humanness I believe is discovered fully, totally, and wonderfully in the person
of Jesus. There is always an invitation on the lips of Jesus to approach him
and to follow him, and in following him, to discover our humanity. "Learn
from me," Jesus declares to weary, burdened, and worn out people;[1] learn

---

1. "Come to me, all you that are weary and carry heavy burdens, and I will give you

from him what it is to be human, humans who are created in the image of God. This is not a book, however, about becoming perfect or successful or trouble free; it is about becoming human in light of the True Human, Jesus Christ. If you are asking questions about what it means to *be human,* I hope you pick up something of value. I doubt that much (if any) of what I say in this book will be unique, for there is nothing new under the sun.[2] I do hope, however, that what I say, while not unique, will be said uniquely. But of far greater importance is that through what is written here the uniqueness of Jesus Christ will be evident. I believe that Jesus reveals to us the truth of who God is and who we are. I believe Jesus is the hope of humanity and the whole cosmos, and what it means to be human is discovered and revealed through him. My humble hope from this book is to enable us to see what it means to be truly human as we encounter the True Human, Jesus Christ.

My sincere belief is that there is much that strips people of their humanity, behavior and attitudes, that lead to dehumanization, to the viewing of others as less than human. Dehumanization not only leads to viewing others as sub-human but also directly impacts the view of our own humanity. Without this realization we can all too easily find our lives lived in sub-human ways whereby we believe the sub-human narrative we are fed by the culture we inhabit in regard to who we are. Within these pages I will examine and explore the ways, ideas, and attitudes that lead to dehumanization that in turn leads to destructive and broken relationships, with ourselves, with others, and with God. And I will return to this theme of relationships again and again throughout these pages, for it is my belief that humanity can only be understood and known through relationship. We are who we are because of those who we are in relationship with, because of others we have shared our lives with, for good or for ill.

What I will not be doing is creating a manual to live by, a Christian behavior code, or rules to live according to. This will not be a book about becoming perfect, for being perfect is not our goal, at least not in the way we often perceive it to be. There will undoubtedly be those who will now quote me the words of Jesus, "Be perfect, therefore, as your heavenly Father is perfect" (Matt 5:48). Michael Hardin makes the interesting point that in Luke's gospel the phrase becomes "Be merciful, just as your Father is

rest. Take my yoke upon you, and learn from me; for I am gentle and humble in heart, and you will find rest for your souls. For my yoke is easy and my burden is light." Matt 11:28–30.

2. "What has been is what will be, and what is done is what will be done; there is nothing new under the sun." Eccl 1:9.

merciful" (Luke 6:36), and in light of Jesus' consistent teaching on mercy throughout the Sermon on the Mount, "to be merciful is to be perfect; to be perfect is to be merciful."[3] Gregory of Nyssa (c.335-c.394) believed that it was "impossible for those who pursue the life of virtue to attain perfection".[4] To those who believe that Christianity is ultimately about holiness codes and morality, this statement will be somewhat jarring. Gregory of Nyssa goes on to explain his thinking:

> The Divine One is himself the Good . . . whose very nature is goodness . . . this good has no limit . . . but stretches out with the limitless. It is therefore undoubtedly impossible to attain perfection, since, as I have said, perfection is not marked off by limits. . . . How, then, would one arrive at the sought-for boundary when he can find no boundary?[5]

What Gregory is saying here is that perfection "stretches out with the limitless" and has no stopping place, no boundary, because perfection is not a "thing," not something that can be attained, not a mode of behaviour; rather, it is "The Divine One," Father, Son, and Spirit. Perfection, then, is not a goal of behavior but is found in relationship—relationship with God. When Christianity becomes a code of morality, an ethic of "right or wrong," then you can be sure that we have ceased following Jesus faithfully, have abandoned relationship with God and each other, and have begun the futile search for "the ghost of perfection."

The Way of life with God is not about "not breaking the rules" but about how we might live lives that ever more reflect the Light and Life of Jesus; how might we become more human. A morality-code Christianity inevitably leads to individualism and how "I" am saved through right living and how "my" salvation is the most important element of my existence. A life like this leads us away from right relationships and is not the abundant life that Jesus calls us into; it is not the life of communion with the Trinitarian Life. Living through a lens of "not breaking the rules" leads to a spirit of judgment and condemnation or perpetual guilt and shame, sometimes both. Why?

> Because for Jesus, holiness is not a solution but a problem. Holiness caused strapping and exclusion; mercy brought reconciliation

3. Hardin, *The Jesus Driven Life*, 82.

4. Gregory of Nyssa, *The Life of Moses*, 5.

5. Ibid, 5–6.

and re-socialization. Holiness depended on graduation and hier-archy; mercy broke through all barriers.[6]

The Way of Jesus is relational, life lived together. "Jesus provides us with a model not of individualism, but of imitation of God."[7] It is to discover Father, Son, and Spirit and his life for us within the context of community, community with God and with one another. It is a community of people who trust together to love one another, bear one another, forgive one an-other, instruct one another, and reinforce one another's witness. Within this Way of discipleship we are not on our own, trying to work it out with me and myself, but living authentically in community—aware of our own weaknesses, aware of the weaknesses of others, and learning together how the Light of Christ might not be dimmed within us but shine ever more brightly to the world around us. This Jesus community is not for heroic per-sonalities trying to go it alone or fix things, but in its vulnerable shared life we foretaste the Kingdom of God. The love of God is non-coercive, non-manipulative, non-violent, and unconditional. A community of disciples seeks to express this Trinitarian love faithfully, not through "rule keeping" but through our common life together, following the Way of Jesus, partici-pants in this peculiar way of life with God, instruments used by God, in the power of the Spirit, to be a people of grace, a people of the cross, a people of God. Jesus has come to humanity full of grace and truth; humanity does not need more rules from church or culture on how to live the perfect life. We do not need prohibitions and holiness codes; humanity needs grace. With greater grace comes greater truth, and with greater truth we discover a more truthful humanity; with greater truth we encounter the One who is Truth.

Some of what I share here within these pages may not be received well; indeed, there may be those reading this who may sincerely struggle with the avenues I lead you down. But I hope that you will persevere to the end and discover something that reveals to you to a truthful vision of who God is and the humanity we are searching for, indeed, the humanity we are beckoned towards.

Slavoj Žižek writes,

> In this new global order, religion has two possible roles: *therapeu-tic* or *critical*. It either helps individuals to function better in the

6. Hardin, *The Jesus Driven Life*, 81.

7. Hardin, *Reading the Bible with René Girard*, 163.

existing order, or it tries to assert itself as a critical agency articulating what is wrong with this order as such, a space for the voices of discontent—in this second case, religion *as such* tends toward assuming the role of a heresy.[8]

I believe that this is the reality for Christianity in the 21st Century. My prayer is that through these pages we might together celebrate the God of history who "dwelled among us" in the Person of Jesus of Nazareth. My hope is for our theological canvases to be painted with a vision of humanity that is faithful to the person of Jesus, to the God who has been revealed in and through him, that together we might see a vision of humanity that is captivating for all around us, whoever we are, whatever our belief system, because the ghost of perfection lurks, haunting us with visions of humanity that leave us groping in the dark. May the Light of the World rouse us from our slumber, from the ghostly dreams that strip away our humanity, leaving us shivering in fear, and may the warmth of his resurrection life bring us to ourselves as we are brought to him.

8. Žižek, *Puppet and the Dwarf*, 3.

Chapter 1

Mission

The ontological fallacy of expecting a light at the end of the tunnel, well, that's
what the preacher sells, same as a shrink. See, the preacher, he encourages your
capacity for illusion. Then he tells you it's a . . . virtue. Always a buck to be had
doing that, and it's such a desperate sense of entitlement, isn't it?

RUST COHLE, *TRUE DETECTIVE*

The decline of church attendance in the West has resulted in the church
spending increasing amounts of time and money in order to sit up and
take notice of why people are leaving and what can be done to reverse the
current trend.[1] Programs of evangelism and mission, books, seminars, seeker
sensitive services, emerging church, Fresh Expressions, Café church, and the
rest are all a reaction to this decline and a genuine desire to do something
positive in order that the church might be properly engaged with and within
our communities, seeking to make known the person of Jesus Christ in ways
that are able to connect with those who are not regularly part of our churches.
Some things have had a positive impact, while some have fallen by the way-
side; but they have mostly come from a heartfelt response to the reality of
church decline and a burden to share the Life of God with others. But there

1. "In 2013, there were 5.4 million church members in the UK, 10% of the adult
population, taken as 15 and over, 300,000 fewer than five years previously in 2008, when
it was 12%. It is likely to continue to decline at about the same rate for the next 12 years,
reaching 9% by 2020 and 8% by 2025, if present trends continue." See http://www.the-
guardian.com/world/2014/jun/03/church-attendance-propped-immigrants-study

is a very real danger that, in the midst of all this desire to reverse the steady decline of church attendance since the 1950s, we subconsciously turn people into "targets" of mission. In subtle and often unconscious ways people can become a "thing" that we are trying to "engage" in order that they would become a part of the church. We want to see results, a change to the situation, so we hope to get a lock on the target, engage our gospel guns, and see mission accomplished. Before we know it we have become obsessed with numbers and have dehumanized the very people we desire to become more human. It is not uncommon for churches to have "vision statements," "smart goals," and "strategies." We hear of how we want ten, twenty, a thousand new people in the church by yesterday. The challenge we face is that when church is about numbers, people become a target, stripped of their identity and humanness and forced into arbitrary categories of "in-ness" and "out-ness." Mission becomes goal-oriented rather than the people of God seeking to show the effervescent display of how God is in Christ reconciling the world to himself.[2]

Although fear is a powerful motivator (think, for instance, how many different types of insurance we "need"), this should never be the driving force behind church activity. Perfect love casts out fear! If fear of church decline and death motivates us, we will discover ourselves hosting event after event, running program after program, desperately trying to grow the church and see results. Our churches are, to use a phrase coined by Rowan Williams, a "mixed economy," different people with different gifts giving their time and energy to enable the church to adequately succeed in achieving its stated goal and vision. All of the language we use throughout the process of realizing our vision would seek to root it in a desire to do the will of God and see no one perish,[3] and I am convinced that most, if not all people involved would be doing it from a genuine desire to see the church grow and people experience the reality of the love of Christ for themselves. Yet behind it all I also believe we have an unconscious problem of dehumanization.

NUMBER GAMES

The motivation of the church in mission can all too easily be about how many people are attending our church service on any given Sunday. This

---

2. " . . . that is, in Christ God was reconciling the world to himself, not counting their trespasses against them, and entrusting the message of reconciliation to us." 2 Cor 5:19.

3. "The Lord is not slow about his promise, as some think of slowness, but is patient with you, not wanting any to perish, but all to come to repentance." 2 Pet 3:9.

motivation of "how many people" could certainly be a means through which the church has a goal and direction, something to aim for, a target to be reached. And certainly the Early Church were not against counting people to see how many had come to faith in Jesus.[4] Yet when "how many" becomes the motivation and mission of the church, it is in danger of becoming a product of a consumerist culture and adopting the same values and motivating features of that culture. Some would argue that this is OK and that the church should define its services just like any secular business would,[5] yet I find this whole concept blasphemous, in that the church is people called together in relationship with God and one another. If the community in which a church is placed is seen as a means through which consumers are targeted with a "product" to sell, and the motivation is to sell a relationship with Jesus,[6] then instead of giving away life, the church is selling a commodity and a product to "fix you up." And if this concept settles too deeply within our church communities, then people become a target; and once that target has been reached, that person inevitably becomes a resource in order to reach other targets, and so the cycle continues. Those within our communities who we are seeking to reach can all too easily simply become "targets" shaped by our vision statements and strategies of growth. People lose their humanity because we become more interested in the survival of our own tribe through the adding of numbers than in the genuine life-giving encounter with the living God. Dehumanizing attitudes run deep and often unconsciously.

Paul Tillich writes,

> Man is supposed to be the master of his world and of himself. But actually he has become a part of the reality he has created, an object among objects, a thing among things, a cog within a universal machine to which he must adapt himself in order not to be smashed by it. But this adaptation makes him a means for ends

---

4. "Those who accepted his message were baptized, and about three thousand were added to their number that day." Acts 2:41 NIV "Probably too much has been made over the claim of 3,000 converts. On the one hand, it could just mean that Luke is indicating a surprisingly large number of the crowd responded positively to Peter's call for repentance, faith, and baptism. On the other hand, the number itself is not out of the realm of possibility. In the first place, the population of Jerusalem at feast time was quite large, perhaps even as high as 180,000 to 200,000 . . . 3,000 would have been a distinct minority of the crowd." Witherington, *The Acts of the Apostles*, 156.

5. "Jesus Christ was a marketing specialist. Like it or not . . . the church is not only in a market but is itself a business." Barna, *Marketing*, 13.

6. See Scotland, "Shopping for a Church: Consumerism and the Churches", 139.

> which are means themselves, and which ultimate end is lacking.
> Out of this predicament of man in the industrial society the expe-
> riences of emptiness and meaninglessness, of dehumanization and
> estrangement have resulted. Man has ceased to encounter reality
> as meaningful.[7]

Here Tillich is making the point that in a world defined by productivity and
success, a reality we created, humanity find themselves defined and valued
in the very same way. People are part of a seemingly never-ending system
whereby their worth is determined by their usefulness or success; they have
become "a thing among things" struggling to give meaning to their existence. So we aspire, we might even say, to find "healing" from the system of
worthlessness that disguises itself in language of worth that is nothing more
than superficiality and sentimentality. So anything that offers us deliverance from the anxiety that all of this produces within us and offers us some
kind of success will undoubtedly be celebrated and pursued. The problem
with this is that so much of what is offered as a solution to the system of
anxiety and despair is nothing more than a reflection back, a continuation
of the very issue we are trying to cure. And the church is not immune to the
complexity of the problem. Dietrich Bonhoeffer (1906–1945) recognized
in his own day the desire for success above everything else, and called the
church to remember what we really are about:

> In a world where success is the measure and justification of all
> things, the figure of him who was sentenced and crucified remains
> a stranger.[8]

The decline in the number of people attending church has resulted in the
very real reality of fractured church communities, disillusionment, and further anxiety. The church itself has become simply "a thing among things,"
recognizing the plethora of objects that offer a solution to the increased
predicament of meaning and self-worth felt by many within society. So the
church unconsciously adopts the identity it has been given by society and
seeks to be the ultimate anxiety cure, the healer among healers, the meaning behind the meaninglessness. But to do that it must be better at what it
does, and so we find ourselves in the place of vision statements, smart goals,
and strategies of growth. But in order for all of this to happen, those who
are already within the church need to be "effective witnesses," using their

---

7. Tillich, "Aspects of a Religious Analysis of Culture.", 106.

8. Bonhoeffer, *Ethics*, 77.

gifts to further the mission of the church. Those on the outside are "targets," and those on the inside are "resources." So when the "targets" are reached and incorporated into the church—the target being a new person who has joined the church—that person in turn becomes a "resource" that we use to go and reach new targets, and so the cycle continues. This circular motion of targets and resources undoubtedly has a knock-on effect upon the depth of relationship within and without our churches. The commandment of Jesus to love one another as he has loved us is part of our highest calling, and we must fight for such depth of love or else see this calling fade away like a distant echo. We must resist the temptation to a shallowness of love for one another within our church communities and beyond, challenging any notion of a church that seeks to grow wider but not deeper in relationship. Mission is a calling into relationship.

PEACEMAKING

Mission, then, rightly understood, is always to first speak of the Trinity, the Father, Son, and Spirit, in eternal mutual indwelling love or *perichoresis*,[9] who *sends* in order to redeem all things from the bondage of death through Self-giving Life; the Father sends the Son; the Father and Son send the Spirit. This redemption and life happen through relationship with the living God, as God alone is the source of all life, and only by sharing in his Life can creatures live.

The North African Christian theologian of the second century Tertullian (c.155–c.230) writes, "The principal crime of the human race, the highest guilt charged upon the world, the whole procuring cause of judgement, is idolatry."[10] In other words, you become what you worship. Idolatry is the worship and direction of our lives towards anything other than God; therefore, if God alone is Life, the worship of anything else will lead to death, since all things one day will decay and die. Mission, at its core, is an invitation into this Life through sign and sacrament, "a sign in the sense of pointer, symbol, example or model; it is sacrament in the sense of mediation, representation, or anticipation."[11] Mission calls people into relation-

9. "This relation is one of eternal mutual indwelling, or 'perichoresis,' as it has been called, rendered possible by Their oneness of nature . . . " John of Damascus, *Exposition of the Orthodox Faith*, 91.

10. Tertullian, *On Idolatry*, 1.

11. Bosch, *Transforming Mission*, 11.

ship with God and displays what relationship with God looks like through relationship with one another. Mission therefore is an act of peacemaking between one another and between us and God.[12]

The Beatitudes,[13] then, are an incredible call to a way of life, a way of life that calls us to be human, a way of life that calls us into relationship with God, a way of life that seems to run at odds to the ways and teachings of society. Indeed, such is their subversive and counter-intuitive impact to our natural tendencies and desires that it is often easier to simply ignore, forget, or even mock these teachings of Jesus as idealistic or fanciful.[14] In a culture like ours that seeks success and growth, the Beatitudes seem irrelevant and completely ludicrous. We are told the strong and confident, not the meek and weak, will inherit the earth. And kingdoms certainly do not belong to the poor and the persecuted. Success and growth have become two sides of the same coin in that we believe that which is blessed is that which grows. But a proper reading of the Gospel will tell us that such an idea is not rooted in the Way of the Kingdom of

12. "'Teacher, which commandment in the law is the greatest?' He said to him, '"You shall love the Lord your God with all your heart, and with all your soul, and with all your mind." This is the greatest and first commandment. And a second is like it: "You shall love your neighbor as yourself." On these two commandments hang all the law and the prophets.'" Matt 22:36–40.

13. "Blessed are the poor in spirit, for theirs is the kingdom of heaven.
"Blessed are those who mourn, for they will be comforted.
"Blessed are the meek, for they will inherit the earth.
"Blessed are those who hunger and thirst for righteousness, for they will be filled.
"Blessed are the merciful, for they will receive mercy.
"Blessed are the pure in heart, for they will see God.
"Blessed are the peacemakers, for they will be called children of God.
"Blessed are those who are persecuted for righteousness' sake, for theirs is the kingdom of heaven.
"Blessed are you when people revile you and persecute you and utter all kinds of evil against you falsely on my account. Rejoice and be glad, for your reward is great in heaven, for in the same way they persecuted the prophets who were before you."
Matt 5:3–12.

14. "Many of the sayings and deeds of Jesus are innocuous, most especially the 'beatitudes' which express such fanciful wish-thinking about the meek and the peacemakers. But many are unintelligible and show a belief in magic, several are absurd and show a primitive attitude to agriculture (this extends to all mentions of plowing and sowing, and all allusions to mustard or fig trees), and many are on the face of it flat-out immoral. The analogy of humans to lilies, for instance, suggests—along with many other injunctions— that things like thrift, innovation, family life, and so forth are a sheer waste of time. ('Take no thought for the morrow.') This is why some of the Gospels, synoptic and apocryphal, report people (including his family members) saying at the time that they thought Jesus must be mad." Hitchens, *God is Not Great*, 117.

God but in the consumerist, materialistic assumptions of such a culture as ours in the West. Jesus' parables that use growth are a metaphor for the kingdom of God, the will and ways of God being established on earth as it is in heaven. Indeed, Jesus also uses examples of pruning, falling away, and even tearing out to illustrate the heart of his Father. All that grows is not necessarily good, and in our desire to be a people of mission we must be careful not to equate growth and goodness. Mission has become the idolatry of the church, with a constant push from all quarters within all denominations that "we" (whoever "we" is) need to be "missional." Again, this is a natural reaction to church demise, but our reactions need to be rooted in that which the Spirit is doing and not based upon our own fears and insecurities. Rather than focusing upon our life together, we are more concerned about growth in number, and such a concern has eroded the very Life of God from among us. Stanley Hauerwas writes,

> We may well have already seen the end of many churches that bear the name Christian while failing to recognize that we have done so because those churches still seem to be in business. But the business they are in may have only a very accidental relation with Christianity.[15]

Modern Christian mission and evangelism, then, often revolve around "meaning of life" strategies that seek to deal with some kind of "lack" in a person's life, which, when dealing with highly prosperous communities, has to revert to emotional manipulation and guilt. Christian ministers become business managers who have to turn around a failing company and so incorporate techniques to make our churches "relevant," "contextual," and "successful." Again, rather than focusing on our life together as an expression and hope of our life in relationship with God, we can easily become a community of sentimentality who have domesticated the faith into something palpable, with mission simply an expression of the projections of a society who are more concerned with individualistic life-style choice than the call to give up all that we are and follow Jesus in the way of the cross.

The Way of Jesus is one where we see power perfected in weakness,[16] where God uses the weak and foolish to shame the wise and strong,[17] where

---

15. Hauerwas, *Approaching the End*, x.

16. "Therefore, to keep me from being too elated, a thorn was given me in the flesh, a messenger of Satan to torment me, to keep me from being too elated. Three times I appealed to the Lord about this, that it would leave me, but he said to me, 'My grace is sufficient for you, for power is made perfect in weakness.'" 2 Cor 12:7b-9.

17. "For the message about the cross is foolishness to those who are perishing, but to

the Son of God empties himself of all power and glory to become human and thus reveals the power and glory of God through his own suffering and death. He is our peace, and peacemakers are called children of God. Peacemakers are lovers and desirers of peace, pursuing the way of peace and calling the world to peace, with mission an outworking and pursuit of Jesus' mission to bring peace. It is the hope and expectation of God's Kingdom. As the book of Isaiah says,

> The wolf shall live with the lamb,
>> the leopard shall lie down with the kid,
> the calf and the lion and the fatling together,
>> and a little child shall lead them.
> The cow and the bear shall graze,
>> their young shall lie down together;
>> and the lion shall eat straw like the ox.
> The nursing child shall play over the hole of the asp,
>> and the weaned child shall put its hand on the adder's den.
> They will not hurt or destroy
>> on all my holy mountain;
> for the earth will be full of the knowledge of the Lord
>> as the waters cover the sea. (Isa 11:6–9)

But peace is not simply the absence of war "out there," but the absence of war "in here," within our very selves. Augustine (354–430) developed the idea, from Paul, that sin was misplaced desire. Thomas Aquinas (1224–74) defined sin as humanity's will being turned away from God.[18] So to be a peacemaker

---

us who are being saved it is the power of God. For it is written, 'I will destroy the wisdom of the wise, and the discernment of the discerning I will thwart.' Where is the one who is wise? Where is the scribe? Where is the debater of this age? Has not God made foolish the wisdom of the world? For since, in the wisdom of God, the world did not know God through wisdom, God decided, through the foolishness of our proclamation, to save those who believe. For Jews demand signs and Greeks desire wisdom, but we proclaim Christ crucified, a stumbling block to Jews and foolishness to Gentiles, but to those who are the called, both Jews and Greeks, Christ the power of God and the wisdom of God. For God's foolishness is wiser than human wisdom, and God's weakness is stronger than human strength. Consider your own call, brothers and sisters: not many of you were wise by human standards, not many were powerful, not many were of noble birth. But God chose what is foolish in the world to shame the wise; God chose what is weak in the world to shame the strong; God chose what is low and despised in the world, things that are not, to reduce to nothing things that are . . . " 1 Cor 1:18–28.

18. Thomas Aquinas, *Summa Theologica*, 2.1.82.3.

is to have the right direction of our affection, namely, to place the will of God above our own wills and desires. Yet very often we desire our own desires above the will of God and the welfare of others. This is why mission that treats people as targets is often simply an extension of our own narcissistic desires that seek recognition for our effort. To be a peacemaker is to desire the betterment of others ahead of our own needs, that they may discover the heart and will of God for their own lives. It is to seek peace for those around you and in doing so see the will and purposes of God displayed and worked out within and through them. Mission, therefore, is a calling to make peace, to "become a people of the last times,"[19] to follow Jesus in his way of peace, to recognize in his life and ministry the reality of the kingdom and the possibility, by the Spirit, to follow him on this same path.

We live in days of violence (something we will examine in chapter 5) and so often struggle to find ways to be at peace with one another and with ourselves. Our violence is not simply physical; it displays itself through the things we say, the way we think, and how we view and treat each other. When a person becomes a "target," we are acting violently towards them, refusing to accept their common humanity, and regarding them as an object that will be used to further our own goals and agendas. Jesus reveals a better way. His death and resurrection uncover the reality that he is the Prince of Peace calling us to be peacemakers in a broken and hurting world, a world disoriented by sin and yet treasured and loved by God. In Christ we see One who does not grasp at equality with God and the glory of Trinitarian life, but humbles himself to the pain and brokenness of human life and yet ushers in through his embodiment of Peace the Kingdom of compassion, forgiveness, healing, and hope. This is his mission that we are called to be part of.

GOD'S FRIEND

As consumers we are conditioned to selfishness, always upgrading our lives and relationships. As Gospel people we are called to servanthood, putting the needs of others ahead of our own, sharing the life and beauty of God who gives his own Self to bring peace to the whole cosmos.

Every act of compassion, justice, evangelism, and peace should be mediated through relationship to reflect a truly Trinitarian model of mission.

---

19. Hauerwas, *The Peaceable Kingdom*, 85.

Without such relationship we are nothing and we gain nothing.[20] Relationship therefore is key, the *telos*[21] of all things,

> This is true perfection: not to avoid a wicked life because, like slaves, we servilely fear punishment, nor to do good because we hope for rewards, as if cashing in on the virtuous life by some businesslike and contractual arrangement. On the contrary, disregarding all those things for which we hope and which have been reserved by promise, we regard falling from God's friendship as the only thing dreadful, and we consider becoming God's friend the only thing worthy of honor and desire. This, as I have said, is the perfection of life.[22]

This is what it means and looks like for the church to grow deeper not wider in mission. It is an invitation into friendship with God, a beckoning of others into this Life, a calling to be human.

---

20. "If I speak in the tongues of mortals and of angels, but do not have love, I am a noisy gong or a clanging cymbal. And if I have prophetic powers, and understand all mysteries and all knowledge, and if I have all faith, so as to remove mountains, but do not have love, I am nothing. If I give away all my possessions, and if I hand over my body so that I may boast, but do not have love, I gain nothing." 1 Cor 13:1–3.

21. *Telos* means purpose, or goal, or final end.

22. Gregory of Nyssa, *The Life of Moses*, 132.

Chapter 2

Triumphalism

I contemplate the moment in the garden, the idea of allowing your own crucifixion.

RUST COHLE, *TRUE DETECTIVE*

In Christopher Nolan's film adaptation of the Batman, Bruce Wayne, having been defeated by the villain Bane, finds himself captured and imprisoned. The prison is a giant hole deep in the ground with prison cells hewn deep into the walls providing the home and final resting place to many criminals. High above, a circle of daylight pours in through an opening that can only be reached through scaling the wall, yet in reality the wall cannot be scaled, the opening never reached. The hope the daylight provides is in truth a poisonous and insidious lie, for it is actually despair,

Bruce Wayne: Why didn't you just . . . kill me?

Bane: You don't fear death. . . . You welcome it. Your punishment must be more severe.

Bruce Wayne: Torture?

Bane: Yes. But not of your body . . . of your soul.

Bruce Wayne: Where am I?

Bane: Home, where I learned the truth about despair, as will you. There's a reason why this prison is the worst hell on earth: hope. Every man who has ventured here over the centuries has looked up to the light and imagined climbing to freedom. So easy . . . so simple. . . . And like shipwrecked men turning to seawater from uncontrollable thirst, many have died trying. I learned here that there can be no true despair without hope. So, as I terrorize Gotham, I will feed its people hope to poison their souls. I will let them believe they can survive so that you can watch them clamoring over each other to "stay in the sun." You can watch me torture an entire city, and when you have truly understood the depth of your failure . . . we will destroy Gotham, and then, when it is done and Gotham is ashes, then you have my permission to die.[1]

Shipwrecked people turning to seawater because of uncontrollable thirst. Seeing the light of freedom but never being able to reach it. This is triumphalism.

Triumphalistic theology could be likened to a dose of drugs coursing through our veins. The initial "hit" provides relief and ecstasy only for the dawning realization of reality to come thundering in again, leaving us desolate and despairing. We could continue to seek another "hit" and drift off again into a state of unreality, or we can expose triumphalism for what it really is doing to us and seek another way.

Triumphalism denies and suppresses the truth and honesty of our humanity in all its joy and its brokenness.

For much of church history, lament has been a vital part of its liturgy, giving "voice to the range of honest human responses and emotions."[2] Lament provides us with an honest reflection of humanity and our experiences, something that is affirmed and echoed throughout Scripture, thus paving the way for discipleship that is truly Jesus-centered:

> He was despised and rejected by others;
> a man of sorrows and acquainted with infirmity. Isa 53:3a

> And they said to him, "Grant us to sit, one at your right hand and one at your left, in your glory." But Jesus said to them, "You do not know what you are asking. Are you able to drink the cup that I drink, or be baptized with the baptism that I am baptized with?" They replied, "We are able." Then Jesus said to them, "The cup that I drink you will drink; and with the baptism with which I am baptized, you will be baptized . . . " Mark 10:37–39

1. *The Dark Knight Rises.*
2. Colwell, *Why Have You Forsaken Me?*, 74.

Jesus, the One through whom the church has interpreted passages like Isaiah 53, is seen to be One who is "a man of sorrows," someone who knows what it to suffer, who calls his followers to walk the way of the cross, to be baptized with his baptism of suffering, to not seek the glory of authority and power—sitting on the right and left of Jesus' kingship—but to seek the Way of his Passion; this is true discipleship. Triumphalistic theology, however, strips us of such a discipleship, and in doing so strips us of our Christ-shaped humanity. Indeed, triumphalistic thinking has led at times to disillusionment with church, abandonment of the faith, and serious ethical concerns.[3]

SUFFERING LOVE

One evening I was asked to preach at an ecumenical gathering, and so I decided to preach on sharing in the sufferings of Christ and how, as a people, we are not only a people of the resurrection but also a people of the cross. On the evening itself there was a time of open prayer before I was due to preach, at which point someone stood up and started to pray about the vision of the new heavens and the new earth as depicted in the book of Revelation. Their prayer then called on God to not only provide the promise of no more tears and crying and pain as a future reality but for it to be a present reality too. They "claimed" this future promise to become a present reality and believed that God could wipe away all pain in this life. I realized at this point that my sermon was not only going to be different in theology to this prayer, it was going to be a different gospel. Yet this is the actuality of the situation we find ourselves in; triumphalism is not the gospel and bears no resemblance to the person of Jesus and his teachings.

Of course, we could argue that this example is extreme and fits more comfortably in the absurdities of the so called "prosperity gospel,"[4] yet triumphalistic theology is far more prevalent than we would perhaps be willing to accept. Take for instance one of the most popular worship songs currently used within our churches,

3. A story emerged recently where a pastor told someone in his congregation who had HIV to stop taking the antiretroviral drugs in the belief that God would heal them; that person died. www.bbc.co.uk/news/uk-england-london-14406818

4. The prosperity gospel is the belief that God desires us to always be healthy and wealthy. If we are not healthy or wealthy, then it is due to a lack of faith on our part. Prosperity preachers thus encourage people to "sow a seed" of money to show an increase in your faith and so "claim" the healing and the money God has stored up for you.

> All the weak find their strength at the sound of your great name
> Hungry souls receive grace at the sound of your great name
> The fatherless—they find their rest at the sound of your great name
> The sick are healed and the dead are raised at the sound of your great name.[5]

I choose this song not because it is *this* song but simply to highlight the pervasiveness of triumphalistic theology throughout evangelical charismatic churches. We have here a concept of God making everything OK any moment now and fixing all that is broken or damaged, whether it is emotional turmoil, spiritual desolation, or physical suffering—any moment now. God is the Great Fixer. The problem with such a view is not only that is it in complete contradiction to true biblical theology, but that it also stands against the testimony and witness of church history. Now of course I want to affirm the God of eternal hope who raised Jesus from the dead and will raise us with him (2 Cor 4:14), the God whom some of the early Church Fathers called the Great Physician, the One who will reconcile to himself all things (Col 1:20). Yet we live in the tension of today where suffering and death are a reality for us all.

Tertullian (c.155–c.230) famously called the blood of the martyrs "the seed of the church," while Dionysius, Bishop of Alexandria (c.200–c.265), spoke of the extent to which Christians cared for the poor and sick, so much so that they "transferred to their own bodies the death that lay upon these."[6] Furthermore, the traditional liturgy of the church followed the Psalter, and therefore lament and a realization of suffering were a regular and honest reflection of life together. Not only that, but the early centuries of the church, marked by suffering and death, were a powerful witness to the Roman Empire that even pagan critics had to acknowledge how Christian believers were a people of courage, compassion, faithfulness, and purity of spirit. Indeed, throughout Christian history there is a rich tradition of lament and a theology of suffering that takes seriously the reality of our brokenness and the brokenness of creation. This is not in any way to speak of humanity as totally depraved or without hope; rather, it is to say that while each of us carries the divine spark, the *imago Dei*, we and all of creation are distorted, "turned backwards";[7] rather than growing

---

5. Words and Music: Krissy Nordhoff/Michael Neale © 2008 Integrity's Praise! Music, Two Nords Music (Admin. by Music Services, Inc.) CCLI Song No. 5393329.

6. Dionysius, *Epistle XIL.*

7. "For, being driven away from Him who truly is [God], and being turned backwards,

into the love of God and seeing it bloom over time, sin sets us ir
direction towards decay and death. And this is an important pc
Too often there is a sense within certain streams of Christian thougu.
our goal is to return to a previous perfected existence, that "heaven" is a
restored Eden. Irenaeus of Lyons (c.130–c.202) had a markedly different
view in that he believed that creation and redemption were intrinsically
linked and that Jesus would not simply restore but enable all things to become something more, something better than they had ever been. With
this in mind he conceives of creation in the beginning being imperfect;
"that makes the fall possible but not inevitable."[8] The imperfection is our
love for God, a love that needs to grow and develop, a love that is not static
and already perfected but increases and flourishes over time in relationship
and communion. Gregory of Nyssa holds perfection to be boundless, not
marked off by limits, for God himself in his nature and goodness is without
limit and infinite; therefore our calling to "be perfect" is a calling to grow in
goodness through relationship with God.[9] Redemption therefore could be
seen as turning around in order to move forward again. To desire to return
to a perceived previous perfected state is to deny our calling to grow into
Christ, who will bring to completion that which he has begun (Phil 1:6).
Triumphalism unconsciously calls people to believe in a magic formula
of perfection and prayer that will enable them to enter into some kind of
super spiritual pre-Adamic perfected humanity. More than this, however,
it is a denial of our suffering. Triumphalism seeks to put meaning to our
suffering and find an answer to why we are suffering so that it might be
overcome or spiritualized; perhaps if I had prayed more, fasted more, spent
more time reading the Bible, gone to church more, had more faith, sinned
less, etc. etc. Even more than that, suffering and death are to be viewed as
a part of "the bigger picture" as though it were simply some part of God's
fatalistic plan that we are not privy to but one day will all make sense. Yet
such a view denies the reality of our suffering, strips us of our humanity,
and makes a mockery of the gospel of Jesus.

    Nicholas Wolterstorff puts it succinctly when he says, "The Christian
gospel tells us more of the meaning of sin than of suffering. . . . To the 'why'

---

he shall . . . continually swim in an abyss without limits, unless, being converted by repentance, he return to the place from which he had been cast out, confessing one God, the
Father, the Creator, and believing [in Him] . . . " Irenaeus, *Against Heresies*, 4.9.3.

    8. Farrow, "St Irenaeus of Lyons: The Church and the World," 348.

    9. Gregory of Nyssa, *The Life of Moses*, 5–6.

of suffering we get no firm answer."[10] Without doubt there is suffering in this world that is a direct result of our own greed, desire for war, violence in speech and deed; but such actions do not give an answer to suffering, merely some of the causes of it. As difficult as it may be, we must not rush to platitudes and sentimentality to somehow seek to give an answer; we must simply sit in the ashes of our suffering and seek companionship, grace, and the whisper of God's Spirit assuring us that He has not abandoned us. There are times when suffering simply *is*; meaningless and painful, it simply is. Although meaningless, it does not negate the possibility that because of Christ's suffering we *might* know that God is with us through such suffering. This does not answer the "why" but *perhaps* enables us to whisper "where" when seeking God's presence in the midst of our suffering and darkness.

PARADOXICAL BEAUTY

Followers of Jesus are told that "the sufferings of Christ flow over into our lives."[11] Without doubt we are participants in Christ's redemptive suffering, and in some mystical way, in imitation of Christ, the church is bound together, fortified, and sustained by suffering together and on behalf of others. Yet this is not an explanation of all suffering. Certainly all suffering and death is taken upon Jesus at the Cross, for "that which He has not assumed He has not healed,"[12] but that does not mean that all suffering is somehow a cosmic balance sheet whereby without suffering there can be no redemption. Such a view would make sacrifice the ultimate cause and effect of all things and so deny the once and for all death of Jesus. The death of Jesus is His uniquely victorious death of which we are participants through God's own divine grace. Death itself does not shape God's love and so somehow be fundamental to who God is, for if it were, God would be like us, "a synthesis of death and life";[13] rather, God, who is love, subverts death and suffering by taking it all upon himself without being changed by it. God does not bow to the power of *necessity* but destroys it, revealing himself to be the one who lives in true freedom.[14]

10. Wolterstorff, *Lament for a Son*, 74.

11. 2 Cor 1:5.

12. Gregory Nazianzus, *Epistle to Cledonius the Priest Against Apollinarius*, Line 73.

13. Bentley Hart, *The Doors of the Sea*, 78.

14. " . . . true freedom is to escape necessity or, rather, to be free to struggle against necessity." Ellul, *Violence*, 127.

We live in this paradox of beauty and brokenness, neither striving for narcissistic utopianism nor seeing complete depravity and hopelessness. Rather,

> To see the world as it should be seen, and to see the true glory of God reflected in it requires the cultivation of charity, of an eye rendered limpid by love . . . the Christian should see two realities at once, one world (as it were) within another: one the world as we know it, in all its beauty and terror, grandeur and dreariness, delight and anguish; and the other the world in its first and ultimate truth, not simply "nature" but "creation," an endless sea of glory, radiant with the beauty of God in every part, innocent of all violence. To see in this way is to rejoice and mourn at once, to regard the world as a mirror of infinite beauty, but as glimpsed through the veil of death; it is to see creation in chains, but beautiful as in the beginning of days.[15]

Thus we are invited by the Spirit of God to see the world and each other with different eyes, eyes that are opened to *see* with realism and hope. Triumphalistic ideology calls us to wear a mask of certainty, believing that we are able to overcome the darkness present around us and so be "fixed." It demands us to be successful, victorious, strong, and powerful. In every way it strips us of our humanity, dehumanizes us, and shatters our faith, for when suffering comes we are simply left with two options: either God has failed or we have failed—both options an apostasy to the life and love we see in Jesus. In Jesus we see the One who is with us, who has not left us, who loves us and walks with us. In Jesus we see the One who carries the scars of the crucifixion into all eternity, whose brokenness on the cross has marked him. The power of the gospel lies not in the "why" but in the "where": Emmanuel, God is with us. Today more than ever, in a broken, a fractured world of relationships, knowing the love for God through the love and companionship of another is vital, and this is where our journey continues.

---

15. Bentley Hart, *The Doors of the Sea*, 60–61.

Chapter 3

Relationships

What do you look at while you're making up your mind? Ours is not a reflective culture; we do not raise our eyes up to the hills. Most of the time we decide the critical things while looking at the linoleum floor of an institutional corridor, or whispering hurriedly in a waiting room with a television blatting nonsense.

DR. LECTER, *HANNIBAL*

Today human relationships are frail, easily fall apart, and are as easy to break as they are to tie together. Electronic communication and social media allow us to have relationships with a safety device: the possibility of instant connection and disconnection. As noted earlier, we live in a consumerist world whereby we are encouraged to constantly upgrade what we have, to get the next new thing and to replace the old. The nostalgia marketing movement that is employed by many companies seeking to sell us their goods is an example of how effective and ingrained an "upgraded" view of the world is. Nostalgia marketing causes us to remember how things used to be, the toys we used to play with, the clothes we used to have, and the way things used to be in our relationships with each other. So we long for the good old days. Nostalgia is a gaze into the "mythical past,"[1] a longing for an object that will fill a "lack," a longing for something that does not really exist but that we create in order to fill a lack or void. Nostalgia is that which we observe from a distance, remembering fondly because we have

1. Žižek, *Looking Awry,* 528.

no way of returning there, forgetting the reality of that distance and any pain within it, and longing in some way for a return to it, even if we were not even born then. Advertisers, politicians, and the powerful are able to capitalize on this nostalgic longing by providing us with those "things" that directly fill our nostalgic desires, whether it be national identity, relationships, wealth, or lifestyle. We can buy cars, phones, toys, and clothes that fulfil our nostalgic desires, creating with them a superficial sense of belonging and discovery of self. The swell in support for the armed forces and Remembrance Day are an example of nostalgia, the belief that through this support we will regain something that we believe to be missing, which, in this case, is national identity.

Nostalgia is, in many ways, what *The Shining* is all about. Stanley Kubrick's classic is ultimately a film exploring the loss of what was, a past that offered so much compared to a present that offers so little. Jack Nicholson's character is haunted by an era long gone, an era "in which an American ruling class projected a class-conscious and unapologetic image of itself and enjoyed its privileges without guilt, openly and armed with its emblems of top-hat and champagne glass . . . "[2] This way of life offers a collectivity among the elite, a way of life that Nicholson's character longs for, a nostalgia that will ultimately be his downfall. What nostalgia offers in *The Shining* is a "knowable community,"[3] and that is what nostalgia offers us today. We can relate to times gone past, reflect on them through rose-tinted eyes, and imagine a time when real community existed.

UNCONDITIONAL LOVE

Films like *The Hunger Games* and *Twilight* and the enduring television program *Friends* perhaps prove to be so successful among teenagers because they imagine a world where the heroes do not quite "fit" and are somewhat loners, yet through discovery "find themselves" through the community of others who do not quite fit, thus creating a new community. Without doubt the growth from child through to adulthood is as unsettling a time in our lives as we could imagine, with a complexity of emotions to contend with, one of which no doubt is a sense of not quite "fitting in" even though all around us are our peers each going through a similar time of change, although undoubtedly unique to them. Films and shows like those above are

2. Jameson, "Historicism in *The Shining*," 82–98.

3. Ibid.

"nostalgic" in the sense that they enable their viewers to imagine another time, perhaps even another world, where they will be part of a knowable community. This is equally true in adulthood, as the success of James Cameron's *Titanic* proved.

Slavoj Žižek argues how the film is not ultimately about a ship hitting an iceberg; rather, it is a story of a "young rich person in crisis who gets . . . restored by a brief intimate contact with the full-blooded life of the poor." The film invites us to "discover ourselves" through the life of Kate Winslet's character, rediscover our identity with her, and restore our self-image with her "quite literally; also, he draws her image." In the film her image, drawn by di Caprio's character, survives, thus furthering the whole premise of self-discovery. The relationship between the two lovers in *Titanic* is seen by Žižek to be "vampiric" in that the poor are merely mediators of self-discovery to the rich and then no longer needed.[4] Perhaps the reason so many of us queued to go and watch this film had nothing to do with its supposed love story and everything to do with a sense of dissatisfaction and desire for change. *Titanic* offers that nostalgic glimpse to self-discovery that society craves, offering to us, this time through "the poor," a knowable community who will enable me to know myself.

The advertisers are well aware of our desire for self-fulfillment and the power nostalgia plays in our consciousness, so they tell us we can have the good old days today by buying something new but making us believe we are simply going back to what we used to have. Now of course we know full well that we are not going back to some previous idyllic life through the buying of any said product, but a belief does not have to be believed in order for it to remain powerful; Santa Claus is an example of this used powerfully by the marketing industry.

Therefore, all we are really doing is upgrading and casting away what we already own. This causes us to be dissatisfied with what we already have and long for something else. Electronic communication along with consumerist culture directly impacts how we relate to one another, and it means that getting rid of the unwanted, much more than the act of getting hold of the desired, has become the meaning of individual freedom.

Our detachment in our relationships is but a symptom of how we are encouraged to become "someone else." Rather than seeking salvation or re-demption that call us to life-long discipleship, we seek instantaneous results of transformation. Polish writer Andrzej Stasiuk puts it like this,

4. Žižek, Slavoj, "A Perverts Guide to Family," lines 34–42.

Applying various techniques, we can change our bodies and reshape them according to a different pattern. . . . When browsing through glossy magazines, one gets the impression that they mostly tell one story—about the ways in which one can remake one's personality, starting from diets, surroundings, homes, and up to a rebuilding of its psychological structure, often code names for the proposition to "be yourself."[5]

Another Polish writer, Slawomir Mrozek, says that the world we live in is like,

a market-stall filled with fancy dress and surrounded by crowds seeking their "selves." . . . One can change dresses without end, so what a wondrous liberty the seekers enjoy. . . . Let's go on searching for our real selves, it's smashing fun—on condition that the real self will be never found. Because if it were, the fun would end . . .[6]

The hard work of depth in our relationships, of commitment to love unconditionally, seems to be something we will continually struggle with if we allow ourselves to be shaped in these ways. Yet we live in a complex paradox of connectedness and disconnectedness. On the one hand, we live in a culture that despairs at the ease at which relationships are so disposable, especially when looking for help in times of trouble, and we live in fear that we may one day be on the receiving end of such endings. On the other hand, that fear causes us to be wary of in-depth relating. We often say that people are looking for friendships, bonds, to belong and be in community, yet I suspect that our desire is more for relationships to be light and loose because deep and committed relationships require hard work and sacrifice. Take, for example, our language and how it has changed from relating and relationships to "connecting," "partnership," "networking," and "being in touch."

Time and again we are fed the concept of new beginnings through upgrading, yet the harsh truth of our time is that of successive endings, never stopping long enough to value people or situations, simply moving on to the next, letting go for fear of stagnation. "Relationship" is understood in terms of satisfaction, success, and results. We want some kind of relationship, yet struggle with the burden it may bring and the limit of freedom it may impose. Social media allows us the perceived freedom to be in control of our relationships to whatever extent we want to be, yet in reality none of us are in control because we are all playing the same game with each other; social media is in control. So how might we navigate some kind of way through this dilemma?

5. Stasiuk, *The Cardboard Aeroplane*, 59.
6. Bauman, "Living in Utopia," line 227–35.

LOVE YOUR NEIGHBOR

To view culture through the lens of biblical faith does not distort reality but offers a high-definition worldview. So speaking to our culture calls us to view the world according to the "theodrama," God's love and action in all of human history. It is to see the world as it is, fallen, corrupted, broken, and groaning to be renewed, yet created good by a good God. This world is not to be escaped like some sinking ship, but for us to pray for God's Kingdom to come here and to see transformation within the communities we live in and in the relationships we have.

Our calling is to the greatest commandments, and this is the most revolutionary, groundbreaking, and sin-shattering way we can speak into our culture. The Christian revolution of the first 300 years after Christ's birth was based upon a notion of love that saw each human as a child of God, that valued every relationship as gift of the divine and revolutionized the entire way we saw one another. Christian teaching from the very beginning placed love at the center of the spiritual life in a way that the world had never seen before and raised the care of widows, orphans, the sick, those in prison, and the poor to the highest levels of what it meant to be a follower of Jesus. The radical nature of the teachings and practice of the church caused the Roman Emperor Julian (A.D. 331–363) to declare, "It is [the Christians'] philanthropy towards strangers, the care they take of the graves of the dead, and the affected sanctity with which they conduct their lives that have done most to spread their atheism."[7] Julian "the Apostate" despised the Christian faith. He regarded the "Galileans" with contempt and sought to bring back the old paganism of Rome to eclipse and eradicate the church. Yet the revolution was now so ingrained within Roman culture that nothing could stop it. What was ingrained was not a set of doctrines and beliefs (although without doubt these mattered), nor was it gimmicks and fads or "new" ways to reach the pagan world with the Gospel of Jesus. What had happened was a movement of love of God and neighbor that literally turned the world upside down. And, as briefly referred to earlier, Dionysus, Bishop of Alexandria, writes, "Certainly very many of our brethren . . . in their exceeding love . . . did not spare themselves, but . . . visited the sick without thought for their own peril . . . cured others of their sicknesses, and restored them to strength, [but] died themselves."[8]

---

7. Julian, *Epistle* 22.
8. Dionysius, *Epsitle XIL*, 108–9.

Depth of love calls us beyond ourselves. It is a calling to follow Jesus, the One who first loved us and gave his life for us. To speak to our culture is to live as agents of Gospel love. This is not some sentimental notion of love but a love so defined by the Trinitarian life, a love defined by Philippians 2 life, by Beatitude discipleship. It is a calling to battle through the clichés and barriers that stop us from truly relating to one another and to pursue unconditional love. It means that we have to put the hard work of relating into each relationship and to view each person we encounter as a child of the living God. It is to not view others as a means to which I will "discover myself" or "find fulfilment," much like the approach to the poor that Žižek points out is happening in *Titanic*. Our call to love neighbor is to actually dwell with neighbor beyond our methods of detachment that are easy to subconsciously be involved in,

> It is easy to love the idealized figure of a poor, helpless neighbor, the starving African or Indian, for example; in other words, it is easy to love one's neighbor as long as he stays far enough from us, as long as there is a proper distance separating us. The problem arises at the moment when he comes too near us, when we start to feel his suffocating proximity—at this moment when the neighbor exposes himself to us too much, love can suddenly turn into hatred.[9]

Jesus sat and ate with people to avoid sentimental, stereotyped, fear-induced relating. In the very act of a shared meal and common table we encounter the Real. Our different ways we eat, the smell of food, talking with your mouth full, spilling drinks, dropped food, delight in taste, satisfaction in a full belly, conversation, laughter—all this draws us into reality with our neighbor, our shared humanity. When confronted with the closeness of the neighbor, such as the prostitute who kisses and bathes his feet, Jesus does not respond in hatred or disgust because of her close proximity; rather he loves her, accepts her, and speaks forgiveness over her. The disciples and religious leaders respond to her in disgust, for she represents the neighbor who has become too close, has invaded our space, and now cannot be observed from a distance.

The parable of the Good Samaritan is a powerful example of who our neighbor is;

> Just then a lawyer stood up to test Jesus. "Teacher," he said, "what must I do to inherit eternal life?" He said to him, "What is written in the law? What do you read there?" He answered, "You shall love

9. Žižek, *Enjoy Your Sympton!: Jacques Lacan in Hollywood and Out*, 8.

the Lord your God with all your heart, and with all your soul, and with all your strength, and with all your mind; and your neighbor as yourself." And he said to him, "You have given the right answer; do this, and you will live."

But wanting to justify himself, he asked Jesus, "And who is my neighbor?" Jesus replied, "A man was going down from Jerusalem to Jericho, and fell into the hands of robbers, who stripped him, beat him, and went away, leaving him half dead. Now by chance a priest was going down that road; and when he saw him, he passed by on the other side. So likewise a Levite, when he came to the place and saw him, passed by on the other side. But a Samaritan while travelling came near him; and when he saw him, he was moved with pity. He went to him and bandaged his wounds, having poured oil and wine on them. Then he put him on his own animal, brought him to an inn, and took care of him. The next day he took out two denarii, gave them to the innkeeper, and said, 'Take care of him; and when I come back, I will repay you whatever more you spend.' Which of these three, do you think, was a neighbor to the man who fell into the hands of the robbers?" He said, "The one who showed him mercy." Jesus said to him, "Go and do likewise." Luke 10:25–37

The Samaritan is the feared Neighbor, *the one whom we are least like, prejudiced towards, and afraid of.* What Jesus does here is challenge our love in relation to our proximity to neighbor. Here our love has to go beyond the distant gaze, the sympathetic nod towards neighbor that may result in my giving some money during Comic Relief, but has to be actually a love that goes to my neighbor and is able to deal with being fully exposed to them and to see in them our very selves, our common humanity, their divine image. Indeed, the power of the Parable of the Good Samaritan is not that we simply have to see our very selves in our neighbor; it is that we have to see our very selves in our enemy, and love them! I fear that much of the angst felt within the Christian community over issues of sexuality has more to do with our fear of the Neighbor's "suffocating proximity" than anything else. In other words, we do what we can to speak in ways that enable us to keep people at arm's length, justifying this with an appeal to Scripture/Tradition without having to be near them. "Love the sinner, hate the sin" is an excuse not to be near our Neighbor. The angst we have towards others stems from the way the Neighbor has come so near to us, is present with us. Indeed, they are washing and kissing Jesus' feet—and our fear turns to indignant rage.

WALK WITH ME

At Christmas we celebrate how the Word became flesh, has now become our neighbor, with God calling us into relationship. Yet too often there is the danger that we handle Scripture in such a way that the text is divorced from the flesh of right relating. Christmas challenges all that we know about God and our common humanity. We encounter the Divine in the hidden corners surrounded by unexpected people. Indeed, God Himself is revealed to us in ways beyond all that we expect, believe and want God to be like—the hungry cry of this newborn into the darkness of the night is the voice of the eternal God made flesh. This vulnerable, helpless child becomes to us our Neighbor. All the emotions, responsibilities, complexities, and challenges a newborn gives to us reveal to us what it is like to love Neighbor. We live in difficult times where relationships between communities are strained through rhetoric, miscommunication, propaganda, and fear. The Christmas story is an example of a time when we are encouraged to be joined together, to re-member[10] our humanity, a humanity gathered in and redeemed through the Christ child, God made flesh. God beckons us around the scene of the first Christmas birth in our shared humanity to a place where all are welcome, where all are equals, where the love of God is seen in the face of those least like me.

From his birth in a cattle-shed to his death on the cross, Jesus fully identifies with the humanity that he created, taking upon himself the limitations, conditions, temptations, and struggles of humankind: the Word became flesh and made His dwelling among us. The Incarnation reveals to us a God who enters our existence, becomes human, and dwells in the reality of our humanness, experiencing our pain and suffering, joy and laughter, hope and despair. In no way does he pretend to be human, but fully and wholly takes upon himself humanity. He walks with us, laughs with us, weeps and wails at death with us. He is tempted and tried with us. He eats and drinks at the Table with us. He is not the detached God who is removed from our lives, but the God who is with us, present in our every moment, loving us with an eternal love. Yet if we are detached in our relationships with others, if we are not willing to incarnate ourselves in the midst of our communities, eating and drinking at the tables of our neighbors, weeping

10. When Jesus says at the Last Supper, "Do this in remembrance of me," it is an invitation for humanity to remember God and remember ourselves and thus put the pieces of our lives back together, to be joined back together in our humanity, a humanity which has been torn apart.

and wailing with them, laughing and hoping alongside them, then they will assume that God is indeed detached and vacant and unapproachable. You are a living witness of the risen Jesus. You are a walking Gospel, good news. I'll say it again: if you are detached in relationship, then people will assume a detached God.

Jesus said that people will know that we are his disciples by the way that we love one another. In the same way, people will have no idea that we are Jesus' disciples by the way we don't love them. They will believe we believe in something, but it won't be in the God who has revealed Himself in Christ. This is a way of life that does not deny the world or seek to escape it like some kind of 21st century Gnosticism;[11] rather, it is a life lived within the world in all its complexity, praying for the effervescent love of God to be lavished upon it.

11. Gnosticism was a school of thought that flourished in the second and third century that taught salvation was attained through a special "knowledge" (*gnosis* in Greek). Although a complex and difficult term to fully explain because of the many and various types of Gnosticism, much of it believed God was detached from the material and physical world, which is therefore evil or defective.

Chapter 4

Fix You

Transference of fear and self-loathing to an authoritarian vessel. It's catharsis. He absorbs their dread with his narrative. Because of this, he's effective at proportion to the amount of certainty he can project.

RUST COHLE, *TRUE DETECTIVE*

Let us be clear: Jesus is not some self-help guru here to make our lives a living luxury. His purpose is not to straighten you out, smarten you up, and propel you into heights of finally fulfilled potential, status, and recognition. He has not set you goals, targets, and a seven-week program to transform you into someone who can stand in front of the mirror and say, "I am beautiful. I am successful." Jesus did not become flesh into the grit and grime of this broken and beautiful cosmos simply to make you the center of it and help you become "a somebody." A life lived with the effervescent God is not to make all your troubles disappear, relieve you of all concerns, keep you safe and sound, or choose you not to die in a plane crash. Dietrich Bonhoeffer lamented our confusion of peace and security saying, "Peace is the opposite to security. . . . Peace means to give oneself altogether to the law of God, wanting no security, but in faith and obedience laying the destiny of the nations in the hand of the almighty God."[1]

God loves you, yes. Indeed, I want to say it again, God loves you! But that love is not expressed in some kind of self-help, fix-yourself lifestyle.

---

1. Bonhoeffer, *Meditations on the Psalms*, 49.

It is expressed through the giving of his Son for the sin, death and corruption of the world and all of creation—beyond our comprehension. This self-giving beckons each of us into his life, having broken the power and slavery of death. He becomes what we are in order that we might become like him, or, as Athanasius boldly claims, "He became man in order that we might become God."[2] Out of context, such a statement can seem almost blasphemous, yet what he is conveying is that through Jesus we are called into the divine life, to be united with God in his life, no longer bound and subjected to death. Certainly he is not for one moment suggesting that we become Ultimate Being, but that we are invited into the Trinitarian dance, adopted as sons and daughters, a people able to call God "Abba," welcomed with great joy into his presence. Our *telos* is life with God; it is relationship with God that leads us into life, dare I say, abundant life. Abundant life, however, is not a spiritualized version of "successful" living; rather, it is a life that walks in faithfulness with the Trinitarian Life, a life that gives to others, a life of self-sacrifice, a life that does not grasp or exploit power but seeks to serve the life of others. It is a life that expresses the lavish love of God through lavishly loving others, raising the lowly, speaking out against injustice, and seeking laughter to break down the walls of despair.

TRAUMATIC CHRISTMAS

Those of us who are followers of Jesus need to be careful that we are not trying to market him and "sell" him as though he were simply the greatest answer to your lifestyle needs, sitting among the plethora of goods designed to transform your life. A Jesus like this is simply an idol filled with empty promises. This Jesus becomes another product for consumers to choose from in order to satisfy their desires. If, in our churches, we are describing a Jesus who will help realize your potential, bring you happiness, and eliminate most of your problems, then we can be sure that this is not the Jesus of Christian orthodoxy who incarnated himself among us and continues to be present by his Spirit. In many ways we have forgotten the trauma of the incarnation, thus resulting in an unrealistic, safe, and sterile version of

---

2. Athanasius, *On the Incarnation*, 8.54. "Athanasius's aphorism . . . while indeed true just as it stands, can be misleading out of its context. Irenaeus can supply the needed precision: the God who becomes what we are is the God-man; what he becomes is what we actually are, 'fallen and passible man, condemned to death'; and we become what he is, humans so united with God as to 'receive and bear God.'" Jenson, *Systematic Theology*, 341.

events. Examine our approach to the nativity scene, a regular event within our churches every year. Consider the "freshly plumped hay and unblemished linen, while in the wings animals look on with wonderment."[3] Such a scene dehumanizes this Christ event and calls us to absurd amounts of sentimentality and triviality. Within my own Baptist tribe it has become commonplace to create a nativity scene in a public place that people are then invited to come and be a part of by dressing up as a shepherd or wise man to then have a picture taken. So we further the sterilization of Advent and perpetuate ridiculous notions of this divine-human event. What this does is draw people away from the gospel, leading them to a false sense of who Jesus is. In reality the trauma of the first Christmas is one where "Christ was born amidst the shit and stench of the stables, like a lotus flower arising out of the mud, a symbol of beauty set against hardship and pain."[4] Now that really is good news! Imagine if we were willing to portray this reality within our churches at Christmas time. This is no "fix-you-up" Christianity, but hopeful reality of how in the "shit and stench" God is at work breathing life and hope, with you, in the midst of hardship and pain.

Yet we live in a cultural climate that has taken upon itself the role of seeking to "fix you," replacing the perceived role of religion having done this before. Without doubt churches and religious communities continue to proclaim such a message; we simply now share it as a dominant theme within culture. Politics, science, media all use language of growth, success, and unlimited possibilities available to us if the conditions are right. In the worldwide film phenomenon *Frozen* there is a song called "Fixer Upper." Some of the lyrics in the song say, "We can fix this fixer-upper with a little bit of love," and "Everyone's a bit of a fixer-upper, that's what it's all about."

Now I do not want to use a Disney film to frame a whole cultural phenomenon, but this does help illustrate something deeply significant about the way Western culture has now shifted—namely, that we are a species in need of "fixing." This used to be language and ideology exclusive to the religious community, yet now we see it all around us in films, television, and advertising, where what we need is to be fixed and "made whole." I am sure many of us have heard sermons and evangelistic talks about how each person has a "God-sized hole" in their heart that only God can fill, or how Jesus will sort your problems out, or some variant of these messages. Now it would be easy to dismiss these types of messages out of hand, yet notions such as

3. Pound, *Theology, Psychoanalysis and Trauma*, xiii.
4. Ibid xiv.

this remain dominant within our churches, albeit sometimes in a much more subtle way. Returning to our earlier point, God is seen to be the Great Fixer, and such a view of God is surprisingly dominant when we reflect more deeply on our theology and style of worship services. I suspect (and I'm willing to be proven wrong) that you rarely hear personal testimony that speaks of fear, doubt, depression, anxiety, loneliness, and the very real sense of God's felt absence, that does not then turn into a story of victory but simply stays in the place of turmoil. Our times together tend to lean towards the triumphalistic and victorious, the stories of how problems have been overcome and of God's victory over various issues in our lives. When pain or suffering come upon us, the language deployed is usually of "attack" by "the enemy" and the need to pray against such assault so that God might deliver us from all evil. Now I am not for one moment saying that God is not intimately involved in our lives, or that God does not care about every part of our existence. I'm also not denying that, "Like a roaring lion your adversary the devil prowls around, looking for someone to devour."[5] What I am saying is that, with a triumphalistic attitude, we always see suffering as a direct result of spiritual attack and the need therefore for such suffering to be fixed.

As stated just moments ago, this attitude towards suffering needing to be fixed has found its way into the secular subconscious. Yet beyond the notion and idea of suffering needing to be fixed is, as the song from *Frozen* illustrates, the idea that we as people need to be fixed. It is fascinating that within secular culture we find advertisers leaping on this utopianistic ideology and thereby selling us the concept that through the acquisition of their product our lives will be made more complete, whole, satisfying, and successful. There are yogurts that are supposed to make us beautiful inside and out,[6] and cars that are reveal to us what real love is.[7] So while some strong

5. 1 Pet 5:8.

6. Activia's strap line is "Feeling good starts from within," while the advert for Perle De Lait yogurt claims that through eating it you will become beautiful with the strap line "Pleasure makes you beautiful."

7. Toyota recently released an advertisement for their new Hybrid car with the following dialogue, "Let me tell you something I've learned. If you're going to do something without love, don't do it at all. Don't stay in a relationship without love; sooner or later you'll realize it's a waste of time. Don't get into a profession you feel no love for; no amount of money will make up for your frustration. Don't cook without love; no matter how closely you follow the recipe, the result will be tasteless. Don't have a pet without love. Don't talk without love. Because no matter how big or how small, if you do things without love, you won't get anywhere. Toyota Hybrid; the reason six million people have fallen in love with driving again."

militant atheistic voices want to celebrate the erosion of religious belief in society, what we actually find is that it is as prevalent as ever but that it now simply finds its voice through the secular scientific community.

SUPER GLUE

Technology and the sciences have now taken upon themselves an almost mythological character whereby if you declare something is "proven by science" then it receives an almost deific status above reproach. David Bentley Hart helpfully points out in *The Experience of God* how, in the intellectual world, there was a significant shift in the early modern period in the way the world and the universe was viewed. The older view saw the physical cosmos as not an end in itself, and so held that a "spiritual" or "immaterial" understanding enabled us to make sense of the whole. Yet views such as this gave way to a view of the cosmos as a giant mechanism, no longer ordered by some kind of mystical indwelling but now a "purely functional arrangement" with "distinct parts and actions."[8] The universe became a mechanism, and humanity, machines. Hart argues that this type of thinking has had a profound effect upon our modern era whereby many assume that if we can discover the physical causes of an object then we can explain in totality the reason for that object.[9] Such is the evangelistic zeal of some within areas of scientific enquiry that they declare how science will one day be able to explain everything,[10] yet a statement like this demands ridicule,

---

What is fascinating with this ad is how it seems to draw directly (or indirectly) from Paul's words in 1 Corinthians 13, yet completely misses the point of what love really is. Instead the ad uses the word "love" to denote a whole variety of human emotions and experiences, yet not all can be defined through a proper understanding of "love." The emotions and feelings I have towards the car that I drive are vastly different from my lived reality, actions, and love I have with my wife and daughters, yet Toyota want us to believe that by driving their car we will discover once again what it means to love properly. The love that Paul describes in 1 Corinthians 13 has nothing to do with sentimentality and everything to do with redemption, grace, unconditional action, the love of God working itself out in the lives of humanity. You can watch the Toyota advertisement here, http://www.youtube.com/watch?v=mtd3hZuzdQM

8. Bentley Hart, *The Experience of God*, 56.

9. For more on this see Bentley Hart, *The Experience of God*, 46–84.

10. Stephen Hawking speaking at Google's Zeitgeist conference in 2011 declared philosophy to be "dead" because it had not kept up with modern developments in science. It appears that Hawking, among others, believes that it is through keeping up with science that the universe's ultimate questions will be answered. See http://www.telegraph.co.uk/

for we have now entered into the realm of the magical and the ludicrous. How can science explain the meaning of consciousness and the way my consciousness is compared to your consciousness? How can science explain philosophical thinking, or the power of love, or the emotion of beauty, or the amazement or horror when dreaming? It cannot, any more than I can tell you who you are through a Petri dish or a microscope.

The effect is, however, that science and technology have become for us the answer to humanity's deepest needs and problems. There is a growing number of Transhumanists who believe that through the advancement in technology and the sciences people can become "better than well," one day "overcoming aging, cognitive shortcomings, involuntary suffering, and our confinement to planet Earth."[11] There are many films that have postulated a future like this such as *Elysium, Transcendence, Lucy,* and *The Minority Report.* All of these films imagine the possibilities for humanity if we can overcome that which "breaks" us and discover ways to "fix" us. Such a view offers us the concept of a humanity without disease or death, suffering or chaos, all through the evolution of technology. While such a view might indeed at first glance appear beautiful, it is in many ways much like the prison Bruce Wayne found himself in: daylight shining in, ultimately producing despair. This is, I suspect, part of the problem we are facing today. All around us we are promised the means to fix ourselves, and so we move from one ideology to the next. We spend our money on every new thing, we join New Age groups and change churches at a heartbeat, we pick up and let go of relationship after relationship, all because we believe the lie that this time this "thing" would mend us, would make us "perfect." Yet we are not created by God to be mended or fixed or transformed into some notion of Western successful, healthy, human perfection. Rather, the gospel offers us a wholly different reality. We are beckoned to become human, a humanity defined in a through Jesus, the True Human.

ONE OF US

In Christ we are not choosing one religious option among others, one lifestyle among others; rather, in Jesus Christ we are seeing the whole cosmos and all reality defined, graced, and judged. In others words, all things, everything, is determined and summed up in Jesus. This means, therefore,

technology/google/8520033/Stephen-Hawking-tells-Google-philosophy-is-dead.html

11. Bailey et al., "Transhumanist Declaration," lines 1–2.

that our reality is determined by Jesus. Without doubt the resurrection of Jesus summons a new reality whereby we are turned from darkness to light, from death to life—but this is not some kind of self-help, fix-you-up ideology. It is an embrace of the complexity of life lived, yet with a new way of seeing. To be a resurrection people means you have to journey through the experience of the cross. While the resurrection continues to be our *telos,* we live as a people of paradox, uncertainty and doubt, complexity and suffering, darkness and death, joy and peace, laughter and love.

To see ourselves in all truthfulness we look at the cross as the Incarnate Son of God takes our place, and in taking our place "it is decided what our place is."[12] This revelation of our place reveals our need for salvation, not in terms of "getting to heaven" or becoming a successful human being, but salvation in terms of complete and total healing from our "sin-sick" state.[13] Sin has utterly contaminated all of creation, and therefore humanity is in need of renewal and healing from our sin-sickness. That Christ fully identifies himself with humanity means that through him humanity may be fully healed and restored from its disorientated and contaminated condition; sin-sickness has a cure. Jesus' identification with us is not about God resembling us and taking upon himself an "outer garment, like a beggar-cloak of a king who dresses up in order to seek out the love of a beggar-girl."[14] It is about God stepping into our humanity and journeying with us through that humanity. Jesus fully identifies with the humanity that he created, taking upon himself the limitations, conditions, temptations, and struggles of humankind.[15] Yet Christ identifying himself with us reveals to us our condition, both good and bad; for in the humanity of the Son we see the goal of all humanity and also recognize how far we have wandered away from the goal that had been intended.[16] Consequently we preach Christ crucified, not consumer Christ. We are a people of Suffering Love beckoning humanity into relationship with God. He became what we are so that

---

12. Barth, *CD* IV/1:240.

13. This is a term Stanley Hauerwas uses to understand humanity as sinners and how this sin disorientates our nature and us. See Hauerwas, "Sinsick," 192.

14. Frost and Hirsch, *The Shaping of Things to Come,* 36.

15. Heb 4:15.

16. "This particular man Jesus Christ, therefore, is not to be considered and judged on the basis of some general preconception about human reality. Rather, every man, and the universal truth concerning man, is to be understood from this particular man." Barth, *God Here and Now,* 6.

we might become what he is. Not so that we become God (*ho Theos*), but so that we might share in the divine (*theos*) nature (2 Pet 1:4).

IS ANYONE OUT THERE?

What we seek then is not a utopianistic ideological concept of being fixed, but a realistic cross and resurrection orientated encounter with God. Therefore we celebrate and rejoice in those times when we see God at work in our lives bringing hope out of despair, life out of death, peace where there was war, forgiveness where there was hate. We recognize throughout the gospels and church history that the Holy Spirit works in powerful and radical ways transforming lives and communities. But we also are aware of the pain and suffering around us, a pain and suffering that cannot always be relieved. Yet God continues to be present, a presence that is affirmed throughout the narrative of scripture, seen powerfully through the story of the Israelites in slavery in Egypt when God hears the Israelites crying out,

> During that long period, the king of Egypt died. The Israelites groaned in their slavery and cried out, and their cry for help because of their slavery went up to God. God heard their groaning and he remembered his covenant with Abraham, with Isaac and with Jacob. So God looked on the Israelites and was concerned about them.[17]

The Hebrew word for cry used here is *sa'aq*, an expression of pain or being wounded, a cry for help, and a question asking if anybody saw: "Will anyone come to my help?" Walter Brueggemann says that the Exodus cry is the "primal scream that permits the beginning of history." He says that *sa'aq* is "a cry of misery and wretchedness" and "a militant sense of being wronged with the powerful expectation that it will be heard and answered."[18] So we recognize the voices crying out in the wilderness asking if God has heard, and with those cries we recognize there are times when heaven appears silent, when our eyes hurt because of the tears, and when darkness appears to be our only friend.[19] God is as present in the cross as he is the resurrec-

---

17. Exod 2:23–25 NIV.

18. Brueggemann, *The Prophetic Imagination,* 11–12.

19. "O Lord, God of my salvation, when, at night, I cry out in your presence, let my prayer come before you; incline your ear to my cry. For my soul is full of troubles, and my life draws near to Sheol; I am counted among those who go down to the Pit; am like those who have no help, like those forsaken among the dead, like the slain that lie in the grave, like those whom you remember no more, for they are cut off from your hand. You have

tion; therefore, we may have to wrestle with times of ultimate uncertainty and doubt where God is silent. Yet in those times God may be more present than ever before. In those wilderness times, moments of complete atheism, God may be more present to us than ever before, for in those moments we no longer have answers, clichés and sentimentality, but the raw reality of our anxiety, fear, and doubt wrestling in the darkness with God's hidden Self. Here in God's felt absence we become more like Jesus and discover something richer and deeper about our own humanity. Here we are not being fixed but are simply accompanied by God in the midst of our pain, not dehumanized by false promises of wholeness but rehumanized by God's presence. In many ways we become worshiping doubters.

Consider this verse in Matthew's gospel: "And when they saw him they worshiped him, but some doubted. And Jesus came to them and said . . ."[20] This is a fascinating verse in Scripture that invites us not to be "fixed" of our uncertainty or lack of faith, but to doubt. Jesus comes to worshipers/doubters/worshiping doubters and sends them all into a world of certainty with the Gospel. Worshiping doubters are sent by God to those who are certain and secure in all that they believe, to declare that they have witnessed something that they do not quite know how to explain or put into words. Oh, they will use words, at times with great confidence; yet those words do not quite portray everything that they have seen and heard. Worshiping doubters declare to a world of certainty and fix-you-up messages that all that they are certain of may need to be re-examined. The resurrection calls us to question everything we know, and invites us to doubt and thus to find faith. Worshiping doubters smash the god idols of certainty that call us to mindlessly adhere to the way the world is. The certainty gods do not want you to think, perceive, and see that you've been lied to. These worshiping doubters have experienced something that has forever changed their lives, but quite how it has been changed and the way it will look in being changed are filled with uncertainty and doubt. They are looking at the Risen Jesus and they do not know how this is all going to turn out. They will go into the world with a message of hope, redemption, and reconciliation, their doubt not a hindrance to their calling but a means through which their calling takes shape. As worshiping doubters we walk unsure of where this

---

put me in the depths of the Pit, in the regions dark and deep . . . But I, O Lord, cry out to you; in the morning my prayer comes before you. O Lord, why do you cast me off? Why do you hide your face from me? . . . my companions are in darkness." Ps 88:1–6, 14, 18b.

20. Matt 28:17–18a NIV.

will all lead, yet that doubt enables us to have faith in God and trust him and not our own strength, skills, knowledge, or wisdom. As a worshiping doubter we find that we can only trust God because we simply do not have the answers. A culture that calls us all to be fixed does not know what to do with such people. Worshiping doubters do not leave their minds at the altar of ignorance; rather, their doubt compels them to think, to pursue, to challenge, and to love God with all that they are. Doubt enables faith and to live in grace. To be a worshiping doubter is to know that the Risen Jesus meets with you, and you have no way of telling what he will do with your life. To be a worshiping doubter is to meet with the Risen Jesus and know that he is beyond your clever ideas, ideology, and understandings of God, yet close to you, present with you, and known by you. The Risen Jesus destroys all our concepts of God and humanity, right and wrong, fear and faith, morality and ethics, life and death; the Risen Jesus compels us to see that everything and everyone has changed in light of his Divine Humanity. Worshiping doubters are called to see God, humanity, and the world with very different eyes and hearts, and to go and be heralds of a brave new world. This journey will be one of failure and despair, suffering without answers, heavenly silence, yet the journey is not to "fix you," but to invite the world into the Divine Life, to encounter the very dance of God, a dance that does indeed beckon us towards a hope and a future, but is utterly real in the reality of Today. Today is filled with violence that ruptures our dance with God; hope calls us to a new reality of non-violence that will beckon us to a different narrative, and it is here we must turn.

Chapter 5

Violence

You have spent years drifting from the light into the shadows and back again, moving between them in your search for answers, but the longer you spend in the darkness, the greater the chance that the presence within it will become aware of you, and will move against you.

THE COLLECTOR, *THE UNQUIET*

In Dostoyevsky's *The Brothers Karamazov*, the character Ivan recalls a poem written in a convent, called "The Travels of the Mother of God among the Damned." The poem describes how the "Mother of God" travels with the archangel Michael to guide her through the various levels of hell, a picture similar to Dante's nine circles of hell. She witnesses the variety of torment that the different categories of sinners endure before finally witnessing those who are damned to "gradually sink in a burning lake of brimstone and fire . . . whose sins cause them to sink so low that they no longer can rise to the surface." The Virgin is utterly shocked and pleads with God through tears to have mercy on all in hell, forgiving and releasing them all from their torment. God, "pointing to the pierced hands and feet of her Son," responds by crying out, "How can I forgive his executioners?" At this the Virgin calls all of heaven to prostrate themselves before God and implore him to change his wrath into mercy and pour out forgiveness on them all. A compromise is obtained whereby there is a yearly respite of tortures and the damned are heard singing,

Thou are right, O Lord, very right,
Thou hast condemned us justly.[1]

It is a fascinating scene within Dostoevsky's classic that highlights how often, even with a call to forgiveness, violent retribution is how many of us understand justice. This is no surprise, as human history has found that violence is the primary means through which we seek to achieve ways of making things "turn out right." The UK and USA's current involvement in Syria, Iraq, and Afghanistan is but one example of how we believe violence to be the only way that we might secure peace and gain security.[2] Violence is a part of our daily existence, yet so ingrained within our sub-conscious that we struggle to recognize it for what it is. Recently I was at a Baptist ministers' gathering, and the conversation and discussion centered upon same-sex marriage and homosexuality. Near the end of the discussion I made a comment in regard to how disproportionate our time was spent on this particular issue compared with, say, violence. One of the ministers said that violence did not really affect our churches, whereas homosexuality did (a comment I disputed with them), and that is why we are spending so much time talking about it and not violence. This comment was an example of how "numb"[3] we are to the issue of violence within our society.

WAKE UP!

Walter Brueggemann in *The Prophetic Imagination* sees the role of prophetic ministry as there to criticize established structures that lead to death and then to energize people through hope. He says, "The task of the prophetic ministry is to nurture, nourish, and evoke a consciousness and perception alternative to the consciousness and perception of the dominant culture around us."[4] Brueggemann asserts that people become enslaved to "the royal consciousness"; society believes that things are simply the way they have to

---

1. Dostoyevsky, *The Brothers Karamazov*, 507–8.

2. Bonhoeffer laments our confusion of peace and security, saying, "Peace is the opposite to security . . . Peace means to give oneself altogether to the law of God, wanting no security, but in faith and obedience laying the destiny of the nations in the hand of the almighty God." *Meditations on the Psalms*, 49.

3. "Numbness" is how Walter Brueggemann describes a society that has become apathetic to the structures in society that lead to death and oppression. See Brueggemann, *The Prophetic Imagination,* 39–46.

4. Ibid, 13.

be. Ultimately the royal consciousness believes that death and violence are a necessary result of the structures put in place to provide wealth, power, and peace. Brueggemann says, "The royal consciousness . . . leads people to numbness, especially numbness about death."[5] He goes on to say, "The task of the prophetic imagination is to cut through the numbness, then penetrate the self-deception, so that the God of endings is confessed as Lord."[6]

Within our own culture here in the West, violence is a regular part of our consciousness. In the movies we watch, the video games we play, and the books we read, violence is often the dominant reaction to the narrative that we are invited to witness and be a part of. A cursory look at the highest grossing films of all time reveals that, in the top ten, most, if not all, use violence as the means through which the world in their own narrative finds redemption.[7] Two of the biggest selling video games, not only in the last five years, but of all time, are the first person series games *Grand Theft Auto* and *Call of Duty*.[8] This is remarkable because these games carry an 18 certificate because of their extreme violence, yet prove to be highly popular, controversially, among children and adults alike. In 2012 the top three selling books in the UK were the *Fifty Shades* trilogy, all of which glamorize sexualized violence.[9] So violence continues to play a significant part in what we watch and read to entertain ourselves. That said, this does not necessarily translate over into our communities whereby we all act violently to each other. Indeed, the link between acts of violence directly as a result from our viewing habits is still unsubstantiated, with evidence both in favor of and against the notion.[10] However, rather than understanding our violence as a result of our entertainment habits, perhaps we should understand our entertainment habits as a direct result of our violence.

5. Ibid, 46.

6. Ibid, 49.

7. See http://boxofficemojo.com/alltime/world/

8. In *Grand Theft Auto* players usually take on the role of a criminal in a big city who has to rise through the ranks of organized crime through brutal and violent methods. These games have been highly criticized for their sexism, violence, and discrimination. *Call of Duty* are first-person shooter games. See www.gamerant.com/call-of-duty-outsell-grand-theft-auto-activision/

9. See http://www.guardian.co.uk/news/datablog/2012/dec/28/top-100-bestselling-books-2012

10. See http://mediacoalition.org/only-a-game/ for a report that argues that violent video games do not increase gun crimes. For the opposite argument see http://www.news.iastate.edu/news/2013/03/26/violentvideogames

POSSESSED BY POSSESSIONS

Advertisers and creators of products understand to a degree the consciousness of the culture. They create and then promote their brands in light of where the culture's ears and eyes are itching. Many advertisers use sex to sell their products because they know that sex sells. Tapping into people's "desire to acquire," they use sex to make people want their product; lust and greed are but two sides of the same coin. Once advertisers have grabbed your attention and convinced you that you need the product they are offering you, it then comes to how long before you go out and buy said product; speed then becomes the form of violence that our lives take. Speed means that we do not have time for one another and that time and space become saturated with speed. By having no time for one another, we put value on those who can keep pace with us and who are able to quickly contribute to the value of our lives. As noted earlier, relationships become an exercise in "target" and "resource," so that you simply become a person I want a relationship with that I might gain something from it.[11] Speed is violence because it has no time for other but is dominated by self, with self-preservation the ultimate understanding of security. Locality becomes insignificant with speed opening up the whole world into each individual home. As Stanley Hauerwas puts it, "The alleged democracies in which we live run on speed, necessitating technologies designed to help us become the sort of people who do not need anyone."[12] Speed becomes the driving force for our possessions, and our possessions the source of our violence. We fear that others desire what we have, "we seek self-deceptive justifications that mire us in patterns of injustice which can be sustained only through coercion."[13] So we become violent to protect what we have. The so-called "War on Terror" after the attacks on the World Trade Center in 2001 has resulted in this very understanding of violence; we assume the giving of violence for the "greater good" will result in our own security and peace.

11. This violent behavior of relationships as commodities is everywhere, but it worryingly is seen within the church. Vision statements made by churches compound the problem because we put a number on how many new people we want to see in the church within the next 3 years. So every relationship outside of the church is seen as a goal towards achieving that number. People therefore become targets to reach. Once reached and inside the church, we then train those achieved targets to become a resource in order to get more targets. We dehumanize each other, making our relationships nothing more than a violent cycle of target and resource.

12. Hauerwas, *Living Gently in a Violent World*, 50.

13. Hauerwas, *The Peaceable Kingdom*, 86–87.

After the September 11th attack, President Bush addressed the nation, and halfway through his speech declared, "Our financial institutions remain strong, and the American economy will be open for business as well.[14] And then on September 27th, 2001, Bush said,

> When they struck, they wanted to create an atmosphere of fear. And one of the great goals of this nation's war is to restore public confidence in the airline industry. It's to tell the traveling public: Get on board. Do your business around the country. Fly and enjoy America's great destination spots. Get down to Disney World in Florida. Take your families and enjoy life, the way we want it to be enjoyed.[15]

Our ability to spend our money on possessions is but another way of us seeking to create our own security and peace. We believe that our possessions will protect us from death, a sign of our ability to have control over our own lives. And so the violence in the world is but a mirror of the violence within our own lives. Our desire for self-preservation means that we will support that which we believe will enable our continued existence, even if that means others perish as a result. After the London bombings on the 7th July 2005, Tony Blair addressed the nation and said,

> The extremist minority . . . in every European city preach hatred of the West and our way of life. This is what we are up against. It cannot be beaten except by confronting it, symptoms and causes, head-on. Without compromise and without delusion. The extremist propaganda is cleverly aimed at their target audience. It plays on our tolerance and good nature. It exploits the tendency to guilt of the developed world, as if it is our behaviour that should change . . . that if we changed our behaviour, they would change theirs. This is a misunderstanding of a catastrophic order.[16]

We have a way of life that needs to be preserved, with politicians calling us to continue to live the way that we are, vowing to eradicate that which would thwart our chosen way of life. Indeed, consumerism is seen to be the answer to the world's poverty problems. David Cameron, speaking at the G8 summit on June 15th, 2013, said that the issues of poverty needed to be dealt with through "the benefits of growth," and that without these growth benefits, poverty will never be eradicated and will continue to cause

---

14. http://archives.cnn.com/2001/US/09/11/bush.speech.text/

15. http://georgewbush-whitehouse.archives.gov/news/releases/2001/09/20010927-1.html

16. http://news.bbc.co.uk/1/hi/uk/4689363.stm

suffering and pain in countries "where thousands of children are dying every day because of malnutrition or where sick parents have to choose between whether to buy medicine to save their own lives, or pay for food for their hungry children."[17] So we are caught in this violent circle where freedom and choice are eradicated, and growth is the god of the age. Poverty is beamed into our front rooms, and charity workers knock on our doors. Rather than being a catalyst for generosity, it becomes something altogether different. We become numb to the violence of poverty, and our language focuses on the self and our own survival; "Charity begins at home" really means, "I'm struggling to preserve my way of life, so give me a tax break and stop helping other countries."[18] Once again we highlight the need for self-preservation.

After the 9/11 and 7/7 attacks, the response from both the USA and UK was of eradicating terrorism. More recently, the murder of the soldier Lee Rigby further emphasized this desire. And certainly most would desire to no longer see such acts of violence and cruelty on our streets, yet when the state calls for an eradication of terrorism, it understands that eradication to happen through the use of violence. So the state believes that violence is the necessary means to preserve freedom and justice. Violence therefore is the normative language of our culture that speaks into our desire to live in our consumerism and see justice prevail. Yet is this the way of the church? Should not the language of those called to worship the Trinitarian God be shaped according to the Word made flesh? Is violence really our only option?

MIMESIS

René Girard (1923–2015) was a French anthropologist who developed the theory of the scapegoat that all violence can be traced back to the system of mimesis (imitation) and mimetic conflict. Humanity, since its beginning, according to Girard's hypothesis, has been violent and has spiraled into ever escalating models of retaliation and conflict. The only way humanity did not wipe itself out was through the discovery of the "scapegoat." This person, the scapegoat, was chosen, usually at random, but based upon their oddness within the society, a person on whom the conflict and lack of peace is blamed. Once the community was united in their condemnation of

17. https://www.gov.uk/government/speeches/prime-ministers-speech-at-g8-open-for-growth

18. I was involved in this very discussion in my local pub recently.

the "scapegoat," that person was murdered in what Girard calls "the founding murder." The "scapegoat" needed to be someone who no one will seek to avenge and that everyone can blame so that there are no repercussions. Furthermore, the innocence of the victim needs to be suppressed, as does the chance nature of their selection, so myths are created surrounding the victim as to their guilt, violence, and cause of violent disharmony among the community. The scapegoat has to be regarded as strange, odd, and odious, an object (important that they are not seen to be "one of us"; otherwise the myth would untangle—they have to be wholly "other" to us) of hatred and condemnation. Yet in their death a miracle occurs: peace is restored, and the group cannot perceive that it was their own murderous mimetic rivalry and so attribute the peace to the victim. Here, argues Girard, is the origin of the gods of religion, myth, sacrifice, and ritual.

Myth arises to conceal the murder and thus project onto the gods divine necessity for blood to bring peace. So powerful is the myth and the collective condemnation of the victim that the victims themselves come to believe the lie and can even offer themselves to "the gods" in order to restore peace to the community. The violence that they have perpetually raged at each other with now finds its totality vented out upon a single victim that unites them in a common purpose and goal. Peace, although fragile, has now been achieved. Chaos has been subdued, and the group can now slowly become something that we would call "community." Killing the scapegoat becomes an act of life for the community, not an act of murder, an act of salvation rather than condemnation.

The scapegoat mechanism is characterized by the following elements:[19]

Mimetic Desire

From our earliest days our humanity is defined, in large part, by learning from, copying, and imitating others. We imitate them (this is what the word *mimesis* means: imitation) by desiring and wanting what they desire. This is not actually a bad thing, as we learn how to speak, walk, and hopefully respect and care for our fellow humanity through this act of imitation and the positive actions and behavior of others.

19. Here I use and adapt Walter Wink's and Raymond Schwager's definition of the scapegoat mechanism. See Wink, *Engaging the Powers*, 145–6, Schwager, *Must there be Scapegoats?*, 46–47.

Mimetic Rivalry

Conflict, unfortunately, also comes through mimetic desire. The person we imitate often and easily becomes our rival as we seek to have what they have and take what is theirs. Suddenly the imitated and the imitator desire the same thing, and rivalry breaks out. Someone then becomes the object of hostility and sometimes violence. Think about toddlers. In a room full of toys, every child wants just one toy, and that is the toy held by the other child. It doesn't matter what toy it is; it is the desire created through the fact that someone else has it.

The Crisis of Distinctions

The differences that separated us are dissolved as a result of us both desiring the same thing, and the social distinctions by which order was preserved collapse. Since humans have a natural tendency towards violence, we pursue violence to solve the crisis. So we seek a scapegoat; conflict can be averted if a scapegoat can be found.

The Necessary Victim

The scapegoat can be anyone as long as they are "other" than us. The scapegoat has to be like us in some way so that we have a sense of affiliation, yet different enough so that we can justify our violence. The fact the hostilities cease after their death seems to confirm their guilt, and "new spheres of relative peace are created."[20]

Sacralizing the Victim

The necessary victim is rendered accursed and sacred through their ability to bring peace to the community. The victim is then given special status, even divinity, as a result. Here, then, taboo, myth, and ritual emerge.

---

20. Ibid, 46.

Sacrificial Repetition

Continual sacrifices of a random scapegoat are offered in light of the victim, but now in strictly controlled scenarios involving ritual and myth, prohibitions and laws. "Internal aggressions are thus diverted once again to the outside, and the community is saved from self-destruction."[21]

Religion covers up the sacrificial mechanism by means of myth, ritual, and prohibition. It institutionalizes amnesia regarding the origins of violence, and endows violence with an aura of necessity and divine ordination that disguises its cost to the victims. Kierkegaard puts it like this,

> The ethical expression for what Abraham did is, that he would murder Isaac; the religious expression is, that he would sacrifice Isaac.[22]

This, however, is the uniqueness of the Biblical story, in that the story that we are invited to hear is from the view of the victim, the one being scapegoated or sacrificed. As we journey through the Biblical narrative, we increasingly see a God who calls for peace, not killing; forgiveness, not vengeance.[23] John Calvin (1509–64) writes,

> Since the beginning of the world there has been no region, no city, in short no household, that could not do without religion, there lies in this a tacit confession of a sense of deity inscribed in the hearts of all.[24]

Calvin is on to something here, and Girard helps bring to clarity what Calvin does not quite see, namely that sacred violence, that sacrifice, is what humanity "could not do without." Ancient communities tore a victim apart in order to stop them tearing themselves apart. Inscribed in the hearts of all has been our need for sacred violence, and it is this "sense of deity" that humanity has been offering victims to "since the foundation of the world."[25] We desire sacrifice to bring us a fragile peace, and we ascribe it to the gods. And in a world of militarism, greed, and racism, not much seems to have

---

21. Ibid, 47.

22. Kierkegaard, *Fear and Trembling*, 41.

23. "He has exhorted us to lead all men, by patience and gentleness, from shame and the love of evil. And this indeed is proved in the case of many who . . . have changed their violent and tyrannical disposition." Justin Martyr, *First Apology*, XVI.

24. Calvin, *Institutes*, I.iii.1.

25. Matt 13:35.

changed. But then Jesus moves into our neighborhood[26] and has given us a new heart, a heart of forgiveness, unconditional love, and we are beckoned to see how God desires mercy, not sacrifice.[27]

> God is love. (1 John 4:8)

> [Love] keeps no record of wrongs. (1 Cor 13:5)

God keeps no record of wrongs and so does not desire sacrifice to placate his anger, for he is not like the gods of sacrifice. The sacred violence is always for us and our anger, and has nothing to do with the God and Father of Jesus. God has already forgiven. It is done. As Jesus said, "It is finished." (John 19:30)

Jesus therefore is the One who reveals an absolute commitment to non-violence, exposing the cycles of violence that destroy humanity and calling people to be defined by another narrative, a non-violent narrative. Indeed, the Cross is a sign and unmasking of all religious violence, revealing a God who will have no part in our violent ways.

AN END OF SACRIFICE

Jesus' life, death, and resurrection "unmasks and thus ends religion based on sacrifice or retributive violence."[28] In the death of Jesus we see the innocent victim get crucified, and we know that this death is unlawful and unjust. In centuries past the murder of the scapegoat would have been justified in some way, and this mythic lie is heard through Caiaphas when he declares, "You do not understand that it is better for you to have one man die for the people that to have the whole nation destroyed."[29] However, in the death of Jesus our eyes are finally opened to the reality of the full innocence of the victim. The story is no longer told from the viewpoint of the collective, the murderers; rather, it is told from the viewpoint of the innocent victim, the victim being God himself,

> The Cross is the supreme scandal . . . because . . . [i]t discredits and deconstructs all the gods of violence, since it reveals the true God,

---

26. "The Word became flesh and blood, and moved into our neighborhood." John 1:14, Peterson, *The Message*.

27. Hos 6:6, Matt 9:13.

28. Weaver, *The Nonviolent Atonement*, 51.

29. John 11:50.

who has not the slightest violence in him. Since the time of the Gospels, mankind as a whole has always failed to comprehend this mystery, and it does so still.[30]

There is no violence in God, no violence desired from God; rather, the Cross is the full absorption of all *our* violence. "In the end, the gospels . . . show that the Love divine must itself suffer in the full most extreme worldly consequences of violence, in order that the lie at the heart of the archaic sacred be ultimately 'nailed.'"[31] In other words, Jesus reveals the lie of the scapegoat mechanism once and for all. Previously the sacrifice of an innocent victim to the gods, although a murderous act, is seen as sacred because it "limits/contains violence, including murder, in everyday life."[32] Žižek continues,

> Therein resides the world-historical rupture introduced by Christianity: now we know [the truth about the sacred], and can no longer pretend that we don't. And, as we have already seen, the impact of this knowledge is not only liberating, but deeply ambiguous: it also deprives society of the stabilizing role of scapegoating and thus opens up the space for violence not contained by any mythic limit.[33]

This is where we discover the paradoxical beauty of it all: Christianity tells the truth about sacred violence, thus rendering it empty of its seductive and creative force, yet leaving us with a very real dilemma as to how we might respond to violence in a way that does not destroy us. Here is why Jesus did not leave us as orphans but gave us the creative means to imagine transformational ways to respond to violence. His command to non-retaliation,[34] to lay down our weapons,[35] and to take up our cross and follow him,[36] is to reject violent cycles of behavior and to embrace a way of life that emphasizes and actively practices non-violence. Yet to live in such a way is at odds with what we have already discovered about the world.

---

30. Girard, *Things Hidden Since the Foundation of the World*, 429–30.
31. Gifford, "Homo Religious in Mimetic Perspective," 334.
32. Žižek, *God in Pain: Inversions of Apocalypse*, 63–64.
33. Ibid.
34. Matt 5:38–41.
35. Matt 26:51–2, John 18:10–11.
36. Luke 14:27.

Consider, for example, the film *Taken*. It has achieved somewhat of a cult status even though it was initially slated by critics.[37] It is a story of a father called Bryan whose teenage daughter is kidnapped and sold into sex-slavery. The father goes on a violent rampage to get his daughter back, killing all who have any part or involvement with his daughter's disappearance. Near the beginning of the film, Bryan is on the phone to his daughter as she is kidnapped. All goes silent, and then we hear the breathing of one of the kidnappers, at which the father utters words that have now become etched in movie folklore,

> I don't know who you are. I don't know what you want. If you are looking for ransom, I can tell you I don't have money. But what I do have are a very particular set of skills, skills I have acquired over a very long career. Skills that make me a nightmare for people like you. If you let my daughter go now, that'll be the end of it. I will not look for you, I will not pursue you. But if you don't, I will look for you, I will find you, and I will kill you.

We find ourselves rooting for Bryan, cheering with every murder, because the people he is killing are worthless and evil. Why should we care about those who kidnap young women, get them addicted to heroin, and sell them as sex-slaves? Is it not better that people like that are dead? Although just a film character, Bryan symbolizes "father" to every parent watching, each concluding that if that was their daughter they would want to do the same to get them back. Surely, then, violence is the only way, a necessary response to the violence of the world around us and the evil that destroys so many lives? There are times when it appears that counter-violence is the only possible and responsible choice, yet for some, like the German pastor Dietrich Bonhoeffer (1906–1945) who was executed by the Third Reich, counter-violence, even under Nazi rule, was not an option. In *The Cost of Discipleship* (written before the Second World War but, in regards to violence, affirmed in his *Letters and Papers from Prison*), Bonhoeffer calls followers of Jesus to "renounce every personal right,"[38] no longer clinging to a perceived sense of rights at all costs, but to be bound to Jesus at all costs. It is in light of this full surrender to Jesus that we refuse "to pay back the enemy in his own coin" of retribution and therefore see that "[v]iolence

37. "Liam Neeson's ill-judged presence should not cause you to even consider going within 30 feet of a fleapit that's screening *Taken*." http://www.empireonline.com/reviews/ReviewComplete.asp?FID=135695

38. Bonhoeffer, *The Cost of Discipleship*, 140.

stands condemned by its failure to evoke counterviolence."[39]According to Jesus there is another way, the way of forgiveness.

FORGIVENESS

Walter Wink calls the way of Jesus "the third way" in direct opposition to the general responses to evil of either passivity or violent opposition: fight or flight. The third way, the Jesus way, is to seek liberation for both the oppressor and the oppressed. It is to declare, in spite of suffering and persecution, that all are equals and that we each share a common humanity. The way of Jesus calls for forgiveness, not retaliation; prayer, not violence; peace, not war; an active opposition of evil, without mirroring that evil. Wink highlights that Jesus does not call for a "passive, Christian doormat quality" but, through non-violent opposition, commands us to find a creative alternative to violence, assert our own humanity and dignity as a person, break the cycle of humiliation, expose the injustice of the system, and die to fear of the old order and its rules.[40] In a time such as this, the church is being commanded to an alternative life to the violent ways of the world, a life that is faithful to the One who called his followers to lay down their weapons[41] and be a people of self-giving love.

> We need to offer our violence to God . . . though not in the manner of those soldiers who allegedly kept their sword hands out of the water when they were baptized. Our violence must go "under the waters" so that the new synthesis, the third way, manifests not only our love but also our shadow. We are . . . wounded, violent, frightened people trying to become human.[42]

Violence destroys our humanity, for in violence we no longer see the person before us as a person but as the "other," the enemy, the one I must destroy to survive. Nonviolence redeems us from mimetic rivalry, from such a way of seeing, and opens our eyes to a new imagination and possibilities. Although people perpetrate so much evil, it is not people whom we fight but principalities and powers, systems that violently enslave both the oppressor

39. Ibid, 90–91.

40. Wink, *Powers that Be*, 98–111.

41. "Then Jesus said to him, 'Put your sword back into its place; for all who take the sword will perish by the sword.'" Matt 26:52. Tertullian writes, "The Lord, by taking away Peter's sword, disarmed every solider thereafter." *On Idolatry,* 19.

42. Wink, *Engaging the Powers*, 294.

and the oppressed. As Martin Luther King Jr declares, our non-violent fight against evil is "directed against forces of evil rather than against persons who are caught up in those forces. It is evil we are seeking to defeat, not the persons victimized by evil."[43] Furthermore, it is a calling by the church to retrace its non-violent history,[44] to seek ways beyond violence and retaliation and to actively pursue peace.[45] Today, with such a dominant culture of violence, the church has an opportunity to be distinct from the "nations" around them, displaying and declaring what it looks like to be a community who practice forgiveness, reconciliation, restorative models of punishment, and frontline peacemaking. To be this kind of people is to be a peculiar and distinct kind of people who are not like the people around them. It is to live—as Israel before were called to live—the Way of the Kingdom of God, a "kingdom run not by . . . strength and connivance but by . . . faith in Yahweh, a servant nation instead of a ruling nation . . . a people set apart, different from all other people by what they are and are becoming—a display-people, a showcase to the world of how being in covenant with Yahweh changes a people."[46] Here we have something distinct and important, that being in covenant with God changes a people, sets them apart as a different people whose attitude and actions are different because they are a covenant people. Therefore, the church is called to be a covenant people with Yahweh made flesh, the One who calls his people to non-violence. At a time of increased worldwide political tension, where demonstrations often break out in violence, where children are exposed to violence in computer games and movies, where in our relationships we act physically and emotionally violently towards one another, to have a people whose way of life is

---

43. King, "Nonviolence and Racial Justice," 120.

44. For a robust and comprehensive account of Christian non-violence, drawing from The Scriptures, Church Fathers, Medieval period, Reformation through to the modern era, see Long, *Christian Peace and Nonviolence.*

45. "At the high meridian of the 'Enlightenment,'" the hope of many was that a world freed from the burden of "superstition" and "priestcraft" would evolve into a rational society, capable of ordering itself peacefully, harmoniously and wisely. . . . And yet, by the end of the 20th century, wars had been waged on a scale never before imagined, and a number of Utopian, strictly secularist ideologies . . . had together managed to kill perhaps 150 million persons. Over three centuries, the worst abuse of ecclesial authority in Christian history . . . caused the deaths of maybe 30,000 . . . but organized irreligion had proved a far more despotic, capricious, and murderous historical force." Bentley-Hart, *The Story of Christianity,* 329–330.

46. Durham, *Exodus,* 263.

non-violent is a powerful and distinct message that points to the God who lives in eternal self-giving love.[47] He is the One who lives in

> the freedom of the Father, the Son, and the Spirit, the freedom of the one who is eternally perfectly loving in this communion and intimacy. . . . God does not need that which is other than himself to love in order to be perfectly loving, he is already and eternally perfectly loving in the communion of Father, Son, and Spirit without that which is other than himself.[48]

To live non-violently is to first recognize our own fear that all too easily dominates our lives. It is to acknowledge this fear and then to learn how to trust again. We need to learn how to trust one another and to see that violence will always erode that trust. We need to trust God,[49] the one who calls for a day when swords will be beaten into ploughshares,[50] who makes wars to cease,[51] and who calls on his people to not trust in war, but to trust in him.[52] To live peacefully is not to believe that we will bring salvation to the world, for that is God's task alone. Rather, it is to live faithfully, prayerfully, and patiently, to, as Clement puts it,

> turn again to the practice of that peace which from the beginning was the mark set before us; and let us look steadfastly to the Father and Creator of the universe, and cleave to his mighty and surpassingly great gifts and benefactions of peace. Let us contemplate him with our understanding, and look with the eyes of our soul to his long-suffering will. Let us reflect how free from wrath he is towards all his creation.[53]

Our task is not, as Stanley Hauerwas has often said, to make the world less violent, but to call each other, the church, to live less violently, that we might

---

47. The doctrine of perichoresis understands God in eternal love and self-giving relationship, Father, Son, and Spirit mutually and fully indwelling one another. This term seems to have first been used by Maximus the Confessor (c.580–662) regarding the divine and human nature of Jesus. John of Damascus (c. 665–/49) seems to be the first to apply it to the persons of the Trinity, although to Irenaeus (c. 130–c.200) and Athanasius (c. 296–373) are attributed the root of the concept.

48. Colwell, *Promise and Presence*, 26.

49. "Trust in the Lord with all your heart." Prov 3:5a.

50. Isa 2:4.

51. Ps 46:9.

52. Ps 20:7.

53. Clement, *The First Epistle of Clement*, 19.

be salt and light in this violent world. To live peacefully is to recognize it is not up to us to "make all things new," that people are not commodities to increase our own status, but that we have all the time in the world to care for those that God calls us to care for. To live peacefully is to live as a people shaped by the gospel, a people who follow the One who declares, "Blessed are the peacemakers, for they will be called sons and daughters of God."[54]

54. Matt 5:9.

Chapter 6

Consumerism

It seemed as if the whole awful creature were simply gorged with blood; he lay like a filthy leech, exhausted with his repletion. . . . Then I stopped and looked at the Count. There was a mocking smile on the bloated face which seemed to drive me mad. This was the being I was helping to transfer to London, where, perhaps for centuries to come, he might, amongst its teeming millions, satiate his lust for blood, and create a new and ever-widening circle of semi-demons to batten on the helpless.

JONATHAN HARKER, *DRACULA*

Friedrich Nietzsche saw a future, painted by Western capitalism, of the Last Men, apathetic creatures with no great passion, no risk or imagination, simply those who pursue comfort and security,

> A little poison now and then: that makes for pleasant dreams. And a lot of poison in the end for a pleasant death. One still works, for work is a form of entertainment. But one takes care not to get too caught up in it. No one is rich or poor anymore: both are too much trouble. Who still wants to rule? Who still wants to obey? Both are too much trouble. No shepherd and one herd! Everyone wants the same, everyone is the same: he who feels otherwise goes freely to the madhouse. "Formerly, all the world was mad"—the finest ones say, and blink. They are clever and know all there is to know: so there is endless mockery. They still quarrel, but they are soon reconciled—otherwise they might spoil their appetite. They have little pleasures for the day and their little pleasures for the night:

but they revere their health. "We have discovered happiness"—the
Last Men say, and blink.[1]

Here we witness a mass of the walking dead, blinking vacantly into the sun
with little regard for the splendor it brings. Their goal is simply to sustain
themselves, feed their endless appetite, and continue on their way towards
no place. All are the same, and those who dare to question the way of the
Last Men are declared to be insane, consigned to the madhouse to utter
their incoherent babble.

Undoubtedly it is a disturbing image of the future, and yet each of
us I am sure feels the knot in our stomachs tighten as we reflect upon our
current Western civilization and see in Nietzsche's vision a profoundly prophetic picture.

Global capitalism appears to be a relentless beast, and we, the consumers, are pulled along blinking vacantly at every advertisement while feeling
an insatiable appetite within to buy something we are not even sure we want.
We are herded along in queues and queues of other people to buy the latest
iPhone or the next *Call of Duty* game or another car or a bigger house. And
each and every time, within moments of possessing this new "stuff," that insatiable hunger rises up within demanding that we feed it again.

ZOMBIES

It is little wonder then that we are fascinated with the un-dead in our film-
going habits, for in many subversive ways they represent the reality of our
predicament. In 2009 Ruben Fleischer directed *Zombieland*, a comedy that
traces the story of a group of survivors of a zombie apocalypse. One of the
main characters, Columbus, explains what happened,

> The plague of the 21st Century, remember mad cow disease? Well,
> mad cow became mad person became mad zombie. It's a fast
> acting virus that leaves you with a swollen brain, a raging fever,
> makes you hateful and violent and leaves you with a really bad case
> of the munchies.

Survivors of the zombie epidemic have learned not to grow attached to
other survivors because they could easily die at any point, so they use nick-
names based on their city of origin. As the film unfolds, a group of four

1. Nietzsche, *Thus Spake Zarathustra*, 12.

survivors bands together, finding in each other companionship, vulnerability, and ultimately family.

The zombie genre has always provided an interesting commentary on various cultural phenomenon, and *Zombieland* appears to be no different. The legions of mindless, soulless creatures whose insatiable appetite needs satisfying are surely a commentary on our consumeristic capitalist culture. What is fascinating in regard to *Zombieland* is how the survivors are each intently focused upon their individual goal, in many ways mirroring the zombie's single-mindedness. However, it is only at the end of the film that they each realize it is relationship that they are really searching for, and this is found in one another. And it is on this point that a book called *Affluenza* is immensely helpful in our discussion.

AFFLUENZA

In this book written in 2007. clinical psychologist Oliver James argues that modern Western society is suffering from rising levels of "emotional distress,"[2] largely caused by the increased levels of consumerism and materialism. He claims that this rise in Western materialism is a direct result of "Selfish Capitalism," and in turn leads to what he has termed as the "Affluenza Virus,"[3] the desire to place a "high value on money, possessions, appearances (physical and social), and fame."[4]

Affluenza, he argues, is a virus of affluence whereby we measure ourselves against each other (notice again Girard's theory of mimetic rivalry), defining our lives and others according to how much we earn, our processions, appearance, and celebrity. The reason for this virus, according to James, is materialism, a desire to "keep up with the Joneses" and find self-worth and value through that which we own and buy—and this materialism, according to James, finds its roots in Selfish Capitalism. James believes Selfish Capitalism to be the form of political economy that is prevalent within Britain and the USA, a term he has coined based upon his

---

2. Oliver James rejects the term "mental illness," saying, "Like many before me, I have come to the conclusion that it is grossly inaccurate to depict depression, anxiety, or even schizophrenia and other psychoses as physical diseases of the body requiring medical treatment." James, *Affluenza*, xx.

3. Ibid, xiii.

4. Ibid.

own understanding of Thatcherism[5] and Reaganomics.[6] Selfish Capitalism has four defining features:

- The success of a company is judged largely by its current share price, rather than by its contribution to society or the economy.

- A strong drive to privatize collective goods, such as water, gas, and electrical utilities.

- Minimal regulation of financial services and labor markets that favor employers and disfavor trade unions. Alongside this are taxes which are not worried about redistribution of wealth but make it easier for the rich to avoid tax altogether.

- Consumption and market forces can meet almost all human needs.[7]

James writes, "Selfish Capitalism cannot afford for us to be satisfied, for that would stifle rampant consumerism and materialistic values, which are essential for its operation."[8] James believes that Selfish Capitalism has been the main driver within contemporary culture in wealthy countries to disconnect us emotionally with one another and so define ourselves according to that which we own rather than who we are, thus valuing ourselves on our material success. The result, according to James, of a "Having" mentality is that we view relationships much the same way as we would view our cars or televisions; they become an object that can be manipulated to serve our purposes, and we value them according to their worth and usefulness for our lives. Relationships are no longer defined by love, but by the satisfying of our narcissistic desires and a feeling that just around the corner there could be a "better" friend or lover. This continued desire for something or someone better is, in James's opinion, crucial for the virus to spread and Selfish Capitalism to continue, because it creates within society emptiness and loneliness that is filled through consumption, which is vital for economic growth, "The more . . . depressed we are, the more we must consume. . . . Consumption holds out the false promise that an internal

---

5. See   http://www.history-ontheweb.co.uk/concepts/thatcherism93.htm   and http://www.leeds.ac.uk/news/article/378/overturning_the_myths_of_thatcherism

6. See   http://www.econlib.org/library/Enc1/Reaganomics.html   and   http://www. knowledgerush.com/kr/encyclopedia/Reaganomics/

7. James, *The Selfish Capitalist,* 120.

8. Ibid, 121.

lack can be fixed by an external means."[9] Commentators on James's work have assumed *Affluenza* is a book highlighting people's varying degrees of happiness, claiming it to be "essentially a treatise about rising unhappiness in modern society,"[10] whereas James himself writes that happiness is not the problem; it is people's emotional well-being that is at stake.[11] As highlighted earlier, we are a people in a system that does not allow us to stop and recognize the reality of our situation, a situation that is not about unhappiness but the assault of "solutions" that seek to anesthetize us, numb us from reality, and encourage us to continue in the system of target and resources.

DESIRE TO ACQUIRE

Consumerism, according to Zygmunt Bauman, "is a type of social arrangement that results from recycling mundane, permanent, and so to speak 'regime-neutral' human wants, desires, and longings into the *principal propelling and operating force* of society."[12] In other words, there is nothing new under the sun,[13] but everything is sold to us as the next new thing that taps into our primal desires. Consequently, society is controlled by its desire to consume, and it therefore continues to invest its money and time into the market of consumerism; this propelling and operating force not only controls society, it blurs the line between needs and wants, creating and changing the value systems of society itself. The consumer market and the pictures painted in the "consumerist utopia"[14] reveal a society that is interested in "solo performances"[15] whereby the importance of "Self" rather than "Others" is highlighted and encouraged, pushing out the sense of community and human togetherness, and creating a narcissistic, egotistic life. It is hard for me to disagree with Bauman, since consumerism has ushered in a time of self-centered individualism that is always concerned

---

9. James, *Affluenza*, 15.

10. Oswald, "Affulenza: A Review," 1. See also http://www.opendemocracy.net/ourkingdom/2008/01/17/affluenza-by-oliver-james-the-blairite-virus

11. "My focus is on why we are so fucked up, not with dangling a false promise of the possibility of happiness." James, *Affluenza*, xvii.

12. Bauman, *Consuming Life*, 28.

13. "What has been is what will be, and what has been done is what will be done; there is nothing new under the sun. Is there a thing of which it is said, 'See, this is new'? It has already been, in the ages before us." Eccl 1:9–10.

14. Bauman, *Consuming Life*, 50.

15. Ibid.

with the wants and needs of "your world"[16] rather than a desire to prosper the community as a whole. Rowan Williams puts it like this,

> Our present ecological crisis, the biggest single practical threat to our human existence in the middle to long term, has, religious people would say, a great deal to do with our failure to think of the world as existing in relation to the mystery of God, not just as a huge warehouse of stuff to be used for our convenience.[17]

In his book James urges his readers to honestly assess whether they actually need a plasma television or brand new sofa, and it is an urge that should be heeded. Yet consumerism is much more than simply a desire to buy new things that we do not necessarily need; it is a force that puts our wants and desires above the common good of society—the "order of egoism"[18] has place in society above the "order of equality."[19] To merely consume what I need is, yet again, highly subjective according to the culture and lifestyle I am already engaged in. Indeed, if "needs" and "wants" have become so blurred, it is highly difficult for any of us to make the distinction. Someone living in the slums of India and someone living in a penthouse in Monaco may have a very different understanding of "needs" and "wants" because of the culture and society they inhabit.

COMMON GOOD

Theologically, perhaps it would be more helpful if we understood what the "common good" might be when we purchase and consume in the society we are a part of. The affluence of one part of society does not mean the good for the whole, and therefore only when a society views the interests of others above the interest of self will our consumption be a means of liberation rather than slavery.

In Philippians 2 we read of how Jesus self-emptied himself in order to be exalted; in humbling himself he receives the name that is above every other name; in his becoming a servant, every knee will bow to him as

16. For an example of this, see the British Gas advertisements, http://www.youtube.com/watch?v=wJRqnjibWyY

17. Williams, "Angels at Peckham Rye," lines 63–67

18. The "order of egoism" is a phrase that is coined by John Dunn that refers to a society that values everything in reference to one's own personal interest; a morality resting on self-interest.

19. Bauman, *Consuming Life,* 140.

King.[20] Here we see the God who does not grasp (mimetic rivalry) at power, but rather willingly serves others, and therefore he offers humanity a vision to be the kind of community that is concerned primarily with the needs of others rather than desires of self. It is a calling to love your neighbor, whoever that neighbor might be,[21] and to put their wellbeing ahead of your own. It is a calling to understand community once again, expressed in the very nature, expression, and action of God,[22] and to seek the common good of community over and against the order of egoism that modernistic society promotes. "The kingdom of God is transformed culture, because it is . . . the conversion of the human spirit from faithlessness and self-service to the knowledge and service of God."[23] The church is called to be a community of such people, a people who see the beauty in one another and celebrate. We must seek to be a people who are able to celebrate our common humanity together, allowing space for mystery, lament, and despair, not seeking to fix, but to walk with you, yet also to laugh and find joy in each other and the world. Fr Georges Florovsky puts it like this,

> Christianity entered history as a new social order, or rather a new social dimension. From the very beginning Christianity was not primarily a "doctrine," but exactly a "community." There was not only a "Message" to be proclaimed and delivered, and "Good News" to be declared. There was precisely a New Community, distinct and peculiar, in the process of growth and formation, to which members were called and recruited. Indeed, "fellowship" (*koinonia*) was the basic category of Christian existence. Primitive Christians felt themselves to be closely knit and bound together in a unity that radically transcended all human boundaries—of race, of culture, of social rank, and indeed the whole dimension of "this world."[24]

Our motives can, however, be a source of selfishness and so challenge this very concept of community. It can be all too easy for us to do things according to how it may be perceived by others or in order to "feel better than

---

20. Phil 2:5–11.

21. Luke 10:25–37.

22. " . . . perichoresis . . . refers to the manner in which the three persons of the Trinity relate to one another . . . an image often used to express this idea . . . of 'a community of being' . . . in which all is shared, united and mutually exchanged." McGrath, *Historical Theology,* 64–65.

23. Niebuhr, *Christ and Culture,* 228.

24. Florovsky, "Empire and Desert: Antinomies of Christian History," 133–59.

others, or to show off, or to manipulate and use."[25] Jesus urges his followers to give to the needy in such a way that your left hand does not know what your right hand is doing; self-glorification is what Jesus warns his followers against, calling them to resist the practice of hypocrites who announce with trumpets the gifts they give to the poor.[26] One of the challenges when giving to charity is when it is so tightly bound to our consumerism. Žižek highlights the modern trend with corporate big business like Starbucks to give a fraction of the cost of the coffee you have just bought to help communities in the majority world trapped in poverty. Žižek makes the point that this has resulted in us being able to carry on with our consumerism while at the same time feeling better about ourselves because some of our money has gone to help a starving child. Yet in reality we should be asking ourselves why people are trapped in poverty and what needs to be done with the system itself that so dehumanizes entire people groups that we consider 20 cents from the cost of our coffee a sufficient way to alleviate the suffering of others.

We need to consider what it is that motivates our desires. Not every charity we give our money to is working out of an ethic and morality code that we might agree to or want to promote. When motivated out of a love ethic, then we are more likely to consider why we give what we give and who we are giving it to. More than that, we will consider how we might live more fully human and work with others to see others' humanity reclaimed and restored.

Theologically and ethically, when Paul writes his first letter to the church in Corinth, he makes it very clear that self-sacrifice and giving amount to nothing if love is not that which motivates the action.[27] The action itself will indeed pass away, but the motivation of love will remain; therefore it is only love that should compel us in our motives. The death and resurrection of Jesus is *the* ultimate event whereby we see the new action of God, who through *these* events is creating a new future for people, creating new identities and a new ethic. To combat selfish motives is not simply to ignore what others may think of you or to perform an action for the freedom of that action; rather, we combat these through the action of the resurrection that ushers in a new history. It is a history that offers freedom for those in slavery, whether that slavery is consumerism and materialism or some other oppressive force, and it is a freedom from oppression

---

25. James, *Affluenza*, 181.

26. Matt 6:1–4.

27. 1 Cor 13:1–3.

that understands itself in light of who God is in eternity, rather than on the basis of being a lone person seeking self-gratification. The resurrection was for the totality of humanity, and it is in light of this motive that all other motives should be understood.

WHAT REALLY MATTERS

The church can easily fall into the trap of seeking to supply the needs of the people and the desires that people have for how church should look or feel and so "potential congregation members ('consumers')" go "church shopping." "Choosing a church is now like exploring the stores . . . in our town and city centers."[28] Affluenza calls us to have whatever we want and to not settle until we have obtained it, and this desire has no doubt become a factor within the life of the Western church inasmuch that we believe that church should be just the way that "I want it" to be. However, life together is not determined by my desires "but rather serves,"[29] finding its purpose in the whole, not simply in its particular context. It is no surprise in an age of rampant consumerism and materialism we have more church "denominations" and "movements" than ever before. Such is our belief in our own ideology that we are willing to sever ourselves from each other in order to pursue and practice our own agenda. Yet as followers of the Way we must recognize how, whether we like it or not, we are mysteriously joined together through the ages and across the world. To embrace a healthy and Christ-centered community is to understand ourselves "as being a part of the one, holy, catholic, Christian Church, where it shares actively and passively in the sufferings and struggles and promise of the whole Church."[30] Consumerism is a reality of modern society, and its effects are far-reaching in terms of government, family, society, and religion. Some might argue that consumerism has brought with it "better health and housing, affordable food, clothing and transport."[31] All of this is true to a degree, yet its truthfulness varies according to the culture in which you live and work. Consumerism may well have brought the UK more affordable clothes, but it has also brought with it increased child labor in the majority world. Consumerism may well have brought more affordable food in the UK through increased importing of foreign goods, but it has also

28. Scotland, "Shopping for a Church: Consumerism and the Churches," 136.

29. Bonhoeffer, *Life Together*, 21.

30. Ibid, 24.

31. Scotland, "Shopping for a Church: Consumerism and the Churches," 145.

caused UK farmers and UK food to be priced out of the market. James's belief that the Affluenza Virus is causing us to be dissatisfied with what we have and instilling a desire for more "stuff" in the hope that this "stuff" will make us happier is hard to refute.

> In our world businesspeople and scholars don't kill each other with weapons. They just kill each other with heart attacks and ulcers.[32]

The church therefore is called to help people find their abundant life not in the cycle of consumerism, but in relationship with God and with other human beings, relationships not defined by what we own, but by the depth of love shown in action. To be woken out of the fantasy world of consumerism and reconnecting "with what really matters"[33] is something that should be pursued and celebrated, for in doing so we reconnect with one another, shattering the dehumanizing pictures consumerism paints of each other. "This is our sin: that we have upended the order of our Creator and gone out to glorify ourselves and to enjoy things forever."[34]

32. Hardin, *Reading the Bible with René Girard*, 186.
33. James, *Affluenza*, 509.
34. Webb, *Conquering the Seven Deadly Sins*, 150.

Chapter 7

Beauty

I think the scariest part was when they took me to pre-op, lying there waiting for them to anesthetize you, knowing that you may never wake again. Actually, what I really remember about that day is driving to hospital . . . there we were driving up Central, and we hit every green light, I mean every single light we hit "swoosh," green. When does that happen? Bang, bang, green the entire way. And the whole time all I could think about was, "Why today? Why can't I spend a few extra minutes in the car with my family? I've never wanted to be stuck in traffic so bad in my life."

WALTER WHITE, *BREAKING BAD*

Jack: [voiceover] We all started seeing things differently. Everywhere we went we were sizing things up. I felt sorry for guys who packed into gyms trying to look like how Calvin Klein or Tommy Hilfiger said they should.

Jack: [looking at a Gucci underwear poster for men] Is that what a real man looks like?

This scene is taken from the 1999 David Fincher film *Fight Club*, an adaptation of the novel with the same name. Jack and Tyler believe that the obsession with self-improvement is a sign of growing weakness, men who have become enslaved to a system of perceived beauty, each of us being cloned into the image of the advertisers—so they begin Fight Club, an opportunity for men to fight each other and find cathartic release from the boredom and clone making structures of society. The character Tyler Durden puts it like this,

> Man, I see in Fight Club the strongest and smartest men who've ever lived. I see all this potential, and I see squandering. God damn it, an entire generation pumping gas, waiting tables; slaves with white collars. Advertising has us chasing cars and clothes, working jobs we hate so we can buy shit we don't need. We're the middle children of history, man. No purpose or place. We have no Great War. No Great Depression. Our Great War's a spiritual war, our Great Depression is our lives. We've all been raised on television to believe that one day we'd all be millionaires, and movie gods, and rock stars. But we won't. And we're slowly learning that fact. And we're very, very pissed off.

Going back to our opening scene, we see a poster of a man with a muscle-toned body, and Jack asks Tyler, "Is that what a real man looks like?" Straight after this exchange we are in Fight Club witnessing Tyler fighting another man. After winning the fight, a shirtless Tyler, played by Brad Pitt, stands up, revealing a body that looks very similar to the Gucci ad in the previous scene. This bit of irony in the film is a great way of subverting our idea of beauty, because Tyler is, in fact, a figment of Jack's imagination, a split personality of Jack that he subconsciously invented in order to escape the banality of his existence. In other words, Jack has created a person within his own imagination who looks like the men in the ads he despises, and thus is desperately seeking to fight the very person he wants to become.

We all know that the images we see on posters, in magazines, and on our screens are not real. We know that they are not real people but computer-generated images, yet so often we find ourselves comparing and imagining our own selves in light of these images. Self-improvement spirals into self-destruction as we never match up to the fantasy that has been created around us. Beauty becomes distorted, each of us subjectively calling out that which we believe to be beautiful yet often finding our definitions defined by the falsity created by advertisers all around us.

Oliver James interviewed a variety of women from a variety of contexts from some of the most affluent parts of the world (Britain, Australia, America, Shanghai), and concluded that most of the women he met regarded themselves as a "commodity which needs . . . bedecking in other commodities."[1] In other words, many women felt they had to compete to

---

1. James, *Affluenza*, 203.

look physically attractive according to the image of the beautiful women they were confronted with each and every day in the media. It should be no surprise then that in many affluent English-speaking nations, people will seek out cosmetic surgery to become more like the people they see in the media, with a desire for greater physical attractiveness.[2] Consequently, we could say that our identity is not something that is given at birth, but, according to Zygmunt Bauman, it is something composed, dismantled, and "born again"[3] by the sellers of consumer goods: "Consumers are driven by the need to . . . remake themselves into attractive commodities,"[4] and their identity is determined by how society sells it to them; identity and beauty is "seeing oneself through the eyes of others."[5]

Now we could seek to understand beauty when viewing it in light of truth. So when an artist paints a picture, its beauty is how close it is to the truth—truth understood in terms of how faithful it is to what is true for you, not according to how it looks through the eyes of others. Unfortunately, we are each a product of our culture, and my understanding of truth and what I perceive to be beautiful is a direct outcome of the culture I inhabit. Therefore, through the onslaught of media, I am already deeply influenced by how they and society understand beauty; and my understanding of what is "beautiful" will change depending upon my culture. I may believe that flying a plane into a building is a "great"[6] thing, or killing a doctor who performs abortions is a heroic act,[7] but that does not mean these things are in any way "great" or "heroic." When beauty is defined according to our own moralistic and personal values, it becomes very elusive and highly subjective. That is certainly not to say there is no such thing as "truth" or

2. People in Britain and America, for instance, had surgery to make their skin look younger; women had implants to make their breasts larger or different in shape; whereas in Singapore and Shanghai women would use cosmetics and even surgery to make their skin whiter so that they looked more Western. A recent documentary by the BBC documented this phenomenon, particularly among the Asian community. See http://www.bbc.co.uk/programmes/boonkpmm

3. Bauman, *Consuming Life,* 49.

4. Ibid, 110–11.

5. James, *Affluenza,* 185.

6. In video footage recorded in 2001, Bin Laden describes the attack on the World Trade Center in 2001 as "great by all measurement." See http://www.telegraph.co.uk/news/worldnews/asia/afghanistan/1362113/Bin-Laden-Yes-I-did-it.html

7. Scott Roeder was jailed for life after shooting dead a doctor who performed abortions in Kansas, USA. A supporter of Roeder said that he was the "definition of a hero." See http://www.msnbc.msn.com/id/36123454/ns/us_news-crime_and_courts/

"beauty," but it is to say that we need to be fully aware of our own context and how we do not "see" or "hear" in a vacuum but as the people we are today with all our experiences, prejudices, beliefs, and traditions.

THOMAS AQUINAS AND BEAUTY

Thomas Aquinas (1224–74) was an Italian Medieval Catholic philosopher who believed that there were three rules that enabled us to determine whether something was beautiful: integrity, right proportionality, and brilliancy.[8] David Bentley Hart helps summarize a Thomist (following the teachings of Thomas Aquinas) definition of beauty well,

> Firstly, a thing's beauty is determined to the degree it is not lacking in any essential feature, and in no way disfigured by privation or distortion; a missing eye or damaged lip detracts from the beauty of a face, a crack deforms the surface of a lovely vase, an off-key note diminishes a bel canto aria. Secondly, all the parts of a beautiful object must be in pleasing proportion to one another; nothing should be either excessive or insufficient; all parts must be arranged harmoniously and in attractive balance. And thirdly, the beautiful thing must shine, must be radiant, in a quite concretely physical way; it must be clear, distinct, splendid, lustrous, brightly colored.[9]

As Hart rightly points out later, such a view of beauty is completely misplaced. While helpful in understanding that which perhaps is pleasing to the eye or technically aesthetically "sound," such a view does little to help us determine the beautiful. Indeed, we may well struggle to find any definition for beauty, because beauty simply *is*. Beauty will often catch us unaware and leave us breathless or in awe. It will grab us when we least expect it, surprise us, and leave us feeling like we have witnessed something beyond ourselves yet within ourselves. Glimpses of beauty will often leave us feeling as though we have touched the transcendent and entered into the divine.

The understanding of beauty as integrity, right proportionality, and brilliancy is so unhelpful—and yet (unconsciously?) this is how modern media society define and sell what is beautiful, and then pass it on to us.

---

8. "For beauty includes three conditions: 'integrity' or 'perfection,' since those things which are impaired are by the very fact ugly; due 'proportion' or 'harmony'; and lastly, 'brightness' or 'clarity,' whence things are called beautiful which have a bright color." Thomas Aquinas, *Summa Theologica*, 1.39.8.

9. Bentley Hart, *The Experience of God*, 278–9.

Today we are bombarded by images of people who are not disfigured in any way, whose faces and bodies are in perfect balance and proportion, and who shine with color and radiance. We may ask ourselves, along with Jack from *Fight Club*, "Is that what a real man/woman looks like?"—yet we know instinctively that such an image is not a picture of beauty but something that seeks to draw our attention, be pleasing to the eye and senses, and convince us of what they are selling, but does not leave us with a sense of wonder, awe and transcendence. We can often find ourselves marveling at something beautiful that is absent of all those things that are supposed to be a definition of beauty. We may indeed discover that our senses find certain things pleasurable, such as the sound of a piece of music or the smell of freshly baked bread; but again, this does not give us a definition of beauty. Without doubt, advertisers depend upon the positive reaction from our senses in order to sell us their product; but again, such a reaction does not define the beautiful. Something may stir my senses and appeal to me and thus draw me to itself, yet beauty points beyond the object, for beauty, as said earlier, simply *is*. Beauty captivates us and stirs our imagination. That is not to say that something aesthetically pleasing cannot point to something beautiful, but it is to say that beauty is not defined by what is technically pleasing to the eye.

Recently a picture was circulating the internet of Pope Francis praying for, hugging, and kissing the forehead of a man suffering with neurofibromatosis,[10] a condition where tumors grow along the nerves. From the photos that were circulating it was quite clear that this man's face and body were severely disfigured as a result of the condition.[11] According to not only Thomist interpretations, but many modern definitions of beauty, this man was ugly. Yet as I looked at these photos I saw something that simply took my breath away and left me feeling as though the divine had come and met with me. I experienced beauty. Pope Francis saw the man for who he is, a child of the living God, and in doing so treated him with the dignity and respect that he deserved. In this picture you see in the face of both men the face of Jesus, faces of radiant beauty that take you beyond themselves, beyond yourself, and yet touch your very soul. The Sufi poet Mahmud Shabestari saw within all things beauty as a mirror reflecting the beauty of God, declaring,

10. http://www.nhs.uk/Conditions/neurofibromatosis-type-2/Pages/Introduction.aspx

11. To view the pictures go to http://www.theguardian.com/commentisfree/2013/nov/08/pope-francis-kisses-disfigured-man

Each atom hides beneath its veil

The soul-amazing beauty of the Beloved's Face.[12]

Beauty leads us into the presence of God and reveals to us the very God who created beauty. Perhaps this is why we find ourselves caught up in something mysterious when we witness beauty, for in doing so we are offered a glimpse of the divine, an invitation into something simply wonderful.

A point of clarity is important here, however. While we may be left breathless at the sun setting over the sea, that is not to say that the sunset nor the sea are God, but it is to say that God is present and deeply involved within all that he has created, and thus they declare his glory and splendor.

BEAUTIFUL WORSHIP?

Far from the deception of photo-shopped pictures, beauty is discovered by the touch of the divine. In the person of Jesus Christ, God made flesh has transformed our understanding of a transcendent God and a created world. The eternal God becomes flesh, thus "infusing the created world anew with divinity."[13] In other words, because of Jesus, creation has been transformed with the promise of redemption, sharing in the wonder of the Triune Life. It is not to say that God changes and somehow creation becomes Ultimate Being, but it does mean that creation shares in the reconciliation of all things to God made possible by the Incarnate Word of God.[14] Humanity and all of creation discovers its true self in light of Jesus:

> In the ministry of Jesus we see the beginning of a titanic struggle against those powers which impede . . . the project of creation. . . . They are actively evil in such a way as to represent a crisis, for they

12. Florence, *The Secret Rose Garden of Sa'd Ud Din Mahmud Shabistari,* 85. The concept of beauty as a mirror is reflected in Sa'd Ud Din Mahmud Shabistari's poem "Every Particle of the World is a Mirror," quoted in McGee, *Haiku,* 105.

13. Coakley, *God, Sexuality, and the Self,* 57.

14. "He is the image of the invisible God, the firstborn of all creation; for in him all things in heaven and on earth were created, things visible and invisible, whether thrones or dominions or rulers or powers—all things have been created through him and for him. He himself is before all things, and in him all things hold together. He is the head of the body, the church; he is the beginning, the firstborn from the dead, so that he might come to have first place in everything. For in him all the fullness of God was pleased to dwell, and through him God was pleased to reconcile to himself all things, whether on earth or in heaven, by making peace through the blood of his cross." Col 1:15-20.

led to the execution of the one who by his activity in all its forms restored the projected direction of the created order.[15]

The darkness of the dehumanizing notions of beauty that surround us can be forced back and eventually extinguished through the One who is the Light of the World, enabling us to see one another for who we really are. Each person is created in the image of God and so carries within him the divine spark that Jesus is seeking to fan into flame.

The church is certainly not immune to false perceptions of beauty, and the dehumanization that is seen within secular structures in regard to beauty can also be seen among the community of disciples. Indeed, Christian marketing, especially within the worship music industry, is fierce. What we have now is a Christian music industry that is extremely slick, looks great, sounds great, and prides itself on excellence. And in contrast many will share anecdotes of their own churches where the music is far from slick, tuneful, or brilliant, and is more of a hindrance to worship than a help. But that is precisely the point. The desire for an experience that will lift you to God (as though God was not already present in the muck and the mire) and enable you to worship is determined by its excellence and ability to stir you emotionally and capture your senses in a pleasing way. When worship music does not do this, we conclude that it has failed to draw us into the presence of God. Why do we believe aesthetic excellence is determinative of God's presence? And is not a pursuit of aesthetic excellence a spiral into an attitude of marketing Jesus as another product that will fix you up and sort you out? Now I am not for one moment saying that God does not and has not met with his people through the music worship present today; after all, "God may speak to us through Russian Communism, a flute concerto, a blossoming shrub, or a dead dog."[16] What I am saying, though, is that this pursuit of false perfection can have a devastating effect upon us as people.

LENS OF PERFECTION

In Darren Aronofsky's *Black Swan* we are invited into a surreal world of dance, paranoia and mental illness. Natalie Portman plays Nina, a shy and nervous ballet dancer in an elite ballet school in New York who is desperate to impress and claim the title role in the upcoming production of

15. Gunton, *The Promise of Trinitarian Theology*, 184.

16. Barth, *CD* I/1:55.

Tchaikovsky's *Swan Lake*. The performance would require someone to play both the innocent and fragile white swan as well as the dark and sensual black swan, which many think Nina would not be able to achieve. Yet she approaches the director to ask for the part:

Nina: I can dance the black swan, too.

Thomas Leroy: Really? In four years every time you dance I see you obsessed getting each and every move perfectly right but I never see you lose yourself. Ever! All that discipline for what?

Nina: [whispers] I just want to be perfect.

Thomas Leroy: What?

Nina: I want to be perfect.

Thomas Leroy: [scoffs] Perfection is not just about control. It's also about letting go. Surprise yourself so you can surprise the audience. Transcendence! Very few have it in them.

Nina: I think I do have it in me.

The film revolves around Nina's desire for perfection, for in perfection she believes she will be beautiful. Yet in her pursuit of perfection, she spirals into madness and despair. The closing scene of the film is of her lying on the stage, having completed the dance and delivering perfection, yet also dying from a self-inflicted stab wound that she gave herself before the show because of her spiral into paranoia. The film ends with her fellow dancers around her initially applauding her and then seeing the blood and realizing something is wrong. Yet she lies there in a state of seeming transcendence and whispers, "I felt it. Perfect. I was perfect."

We must be careful not to allow ourselves to fall into this trap of perfection within our churches, believing that God will only meet with us if we offer a slick and well-tailored version of events. And we must not enter into the game whereby we seek to "get people in" through a well-managed set piece, believing, like Nina in *The Black Swan*, that striving for visual perfection will lead us into transcendent beauty. Beauty lies way beyond such things when we consider "the figure of him who was sentenced and crucified." At the sight of the Crucified God, we discover real beauty, that in the face of every person we glimpse the face of Jesus who is the image of the invisible God, the One in whose image each person is created.

THE FACE OF JESUS

A worshipping community then does not seek aesthetic perfection. Rather, it seeks truthfulness and honesty, recognition of our own selves and our life together in all its complexity, ambiguity, vulnerability, brokenness, and doubt. It is a community that celebrates each person, not based on some kind of arbitrary definition of excellence but on the honesty of facing up to our own selves and being that person together. Here we discover beauty. What many people are actually searching for is authentic relationship, because in authentic relationship we encounter the Trinitarian life, the God of eternal self-giving relationship. In authentic relationship we see and celebrate one another for who we really are. This is where the disabled community speaks to us about beauty. John Paul II wrote,

> There is no doubt that in revealing the fundamental frailty of the human condition, the disabled person becomes an expression of the tragedy of pain. In this world of ours that approves hedonism and is charmed by ephemeral and deceptive beauty, the difficulties of the disabled are often perceived as a shame or a provocation, and their problem as burdens to be removed or resolved as quickly as possible. Disabled people are instead living icons of the crucified Son. They reveal the mysterious beauty of the One who emptied himself for our sake and made himself obedient unto death. They show us over and above all appearances that the ultimate foundation of human existence is Jesus Christ. It is said (justifiably so) that disabled people are humanity's privileged witnesses. They can teach everyone about the love that saves us; they can become heralds of a new world, no longer dominated by force, violence, and aggression, but by love, solidarity, and acceptance—a new world transfigured by the light of Christ, the Son of God, who became incarnate, who was crucified, and rose for us.[17]

Here we have a vision of beauty that is not defined by "ephemeral and deceptive" means but through the life of disabled people, a people who reveal that humanity are a people of all abilities. Here we see that we encounter the divine not through arbitrary notions of excellence but through the mystery and wonder of "love, solidarity, and acceptance." This is not to say that churches should be a place where anything goes, because I firmly believe that as a community we need to ensure all people are properly cared for

17. John Paul II, "Message of John Paul II on the Occasion of the International Symposium on the Dignity and Rights of the Mentally Disabled Person," quoted in Hauerwas and Vanier, *Living Gently in a Violent World*, 38–39.

and safe, so good practice for children and vulnerable people is essential. Therefore, people need to be trained well and be suitable in the roles they take. But this is not the same as sensory "beauty" where everything has to look a certain way. If the church has a minister, then that minister should be trained well, because that minister is ultimately caring for people; but it is the obsession we have for sensory excellence that I believe to be extremely destructive. We need to be a community of people who welcome the gifts and character of each person and allow them to express that. The life and ministry of the church should be developed according to the gifts and passion of the people. It should not be that the ministry of the church determines the gifts and passion of the people, which is the usual way that we do things. Even more than this, the church is a place of relationship, and so we need to be a community of people who eat together, pray together, and celebrate together. Here we discover true beauty. A community like this recognizes the fear, anxiety, doubt, and suffering of one another and learns how to live together with our common pain and tragedy. Suffering, as we saw earlier, is not the absence of God; rather, it may be the place where we discover God. I am not saying that God is the cause of suffering, but that in the depths of Jesus' cry of suffering we hear our own suffering.

Within our churches and within our communities we need to discover beauty, for in doing so we rehumanize one another, no longer defining one another with false notions of the beautiful, but seeing our humanity in light of the crucified and risen Son. John Paul II frames beauty through Jesus, seeing humanity through his humanity. In the book of Genesis we read that "God created man in his own image, in the image of God he created him; male and female he created them." Christian interpretation of these verses will hear in the text Jesus of Nazareth "who is the image of God,"[18] and therefore it is in Jesus Christ that humanity finds its definition, understanding, and purpose. Humanity, in and through Jesus Christ, is offered fresh insight into who God is and who humankind are called to become.[19] Beauty therefore is not understood in light of some outward appearance;[20]

18. 2 Cor 4:4. See also Col 1:15.

19. "For in times long past, it was said that man was created after the image of God, but it was not [actually] shown; for the Word was as yet invisible, after whose image man was created. . . . When, however, the Word of God became flesh, he confirmed both these: for he both showed forth the image truly, since he became himself what was his image." Irenaeus, *Against Heresies*, 5.16.2.

20. "He had no beauty or majesty to attract us to him, nothing in his appearance that we should desire him." Isa 53:2b.

rather, beauty could be understood in terms of who we are called to become in and through the person of Jesus—and how we act in response. Beauty therefore, is no longer about outward appearances or subjective opinions, but it becomes something defined in Christ. Yet this does not mean we can "grasp" it or define it, because we will always discover with beauty, as we always discover with Jesus, that we are surprised, amazed, and at times, simply breathless at what we have just witnessed or experienced. It points us beyond ourselves and yet calls us to a place within. This, I believe, is our path to beauty and the recognition that all are beautiful.

Chapter 8

Prayer

It's what no one knows about you that allows you to know yourself.

RICHARD ELSTER, *POINT OMEGA*

Augustine's *Confessions* is perhaps one of the most widely read works of medieval theology and philosophy within and without the church. Noted for the uniqueness at the time of its autobiographical style, *Confessions* is a remarkable work that has both challenged and inspired its readers for over 1600 years. It is a biography written as a prayer, and is, I believe, helpful as we explore prayer in this chapter.

Augustine had devoted nine years of his life to a religious group called the Manicheans, believing they had the key to understanding the way of the cosmos and had the answers to "the problems which perplexed me."[1] However, it became clear to Augustine that this was simply not the case. His attraction to Christianity was in part that he could not exhaust the theological and intellectual depth of Christian doctrine and the Bible as he had done with the Manichean books. Augustine writes about his meeting with Faustus, a bishop of the Manicheans, and his disappointment with how uninformed Faustus was "about the subjects in which I expected him to be an expert."[2] However, Augustine respected him for his honesty in admitting that "he did not know the answers to my questions and was not ashamed to admit it, for,

1. Augustine, *Confessions*, 98, 5.7
2. Ibid.

unlike many other talkative people whom I have had to endure, he would not try to teach me a lesson when he had nothing to say."[3] This, however, I have begun to see as a problem within the Western evangelical tradition, in that we have plenty to say even though the reality is that what we are saying may not have much to minister into our communities. This having plenty to say but actually having nothing to say, added to the lack of mystery, lack of theological questioning, lack of lament, and intellectual shallowness, has led me to increasingly become concerned that much of what we are saying is "tedious fictions"[4] that are less to do with the Gospel and Kingdom of God and more to do with sentimentality and self-help idolatry.[5] For instance, often the church can fall into the trap of appealing to some universal or general notion of "love" as a way of engaging more broadly and widely with our communities. So we use the language of "cross," "forgiveness," and God," but make our appeal out of a sentimental abstraction and notion of "love" rather than love as defined by the Trinitarian life. An example of this is the appeal to "invite Jesus into your heart/life." A natural outworking of this is that the feelings and understanding of our hearts are how we define our relationship with God and our understanding of God. Furthermore, discipleship then becomes a series of thoughts and habits that are designed to make me a feel a little bit better about my life. All of this stands in stark contrast to discipleship as defined by the Gospel, whereby we are baptized into the death of Christ in order that we might be raised with him (Romans 6:3–4). This baptism calls us to share in the sufferings of Christ, deny ourselves, and be ready to die.[6] The defect in our theology and discipleship is "like trying to see darkness or hear silence. Yet we are familiar with darkness and silence, and we can only be aware of them by means of ears and eyes, but this is not by perception but by absence of perception."[7] Proper discipleship is the call to be more human, beckoned into relationship with God and others. It is a call of the church to see and understand the world according to the Light of Christ, and for God, as Augustine emphasized so often, to be the One whom we desire above everything else. And prayer at its heart is a desire for God, a recognition that we need God, that we are dependent upon him.

3. Ibid.

4. Ibid.

5. "The principal crime of the human race, the highest guilt charged upon the world, the whole procuring cause of judgement, is idolatry." Tertullian, *On Idolatry*, 2.1.

6. See Mark 10:35–40, Rom 6, 1 Pet 4:12–17.

7. Augustine, *City of God*, 480.

GOD IS ABLE

Christian faith from its very beginnings has declared that God is able (Jude 24). Early Christian witness was to a God who not only was able but who was wholly other and supreme to all things. Irenaeus declared that God "is not as men are.... [t]he Father of all is ... a simple, uncompounded Being, without diverse members, and altogether like, and equal to himself, since he is wholly understanding, and wholly spirit, and wholly thought, and wholly intelligence, and wholly reason, and wholly hearing, and wholly seeing, and wholly light, and the whole source of all that is good."[8] God's supremacy over all things and his Lordship over the whole cosmos (Colossians 1:15–18) was powerfully witnessed to and affirmed by the early church in face of fierce persecution and demands upon them to swear their allegiance to Caesar, something that they refused to do; "God is able" was their ringing testimony. However, we live in a time when many would seek to convince us that humanity is able on its own without any need for God. Certainly this is not a new concept, with history littered with human desire to "go it alone," be masters of their own lives, and discover a perceived freedom from religious conviction and faith in God. Many have come to believe that God is an unnecessary part of human life, that our own advancements and achievements have made God an irrelevance, and that there is no need for God. Without doubt our continued discoveries in the sciences, anthropology, and cultural hermeneutics, among other things, have enabled many exciting and revolutionary changes to take place within our societies. Yet as advanced as we appear to be, as able as we think we are, we are left with the reality that, compared to God, we simply are not able;

> Can you bind the chains of the Pleiades, or loose the cords of Orion? Can you lead forth the Mazzaroth in their season, or can you guide the Bear with its children? Do you know the ordinances of the heavens? Can you establish their rule on the earth? Job 38:31–3

Prayer calls us to a dependency upon God, a recognition that God is able, and that we are continually in need of his "able-ness" to enable us to go on each moment of each day. Bonhoeffer in *The Cost of Discipleship* says, "Prayer is the supreme instance of the hidden character of the Christian life. It is the antithesis of self-display. When we pray, we have ceased to know ourselves, and know only God whom we call upon. Prayer does not

---

8. Irenaeus, *Against Heresies*, 2.8.3.

aim at any direct effect on the world; it is addressed to God alone."[9] Yet in an increasingly self-serving, individualistic, independent world, prayer as abandonment to God and example of total reliance upon God is easily sacrificed on the altar of our own abilities. In a viral video for the film *Prometheus*, Peter Wayland highlights the advances humanity has made since the dawn of civilization, concluding that "We are the gods now."

This celebration of our own abilities can all too easily impact our churches in that prayer becomes less and less of a priority. Our ability to "do stuff" well means that we can grow our churches, establish our ministries, and make an impact upon our communities without any real need to pray. Each of us can easily live our life and go about our weekly tasks as though we were an atheist if ministry is simply about getting "stuff" done. Prayer, however, causes us to see that God alone is able. Prayer leads us into the reality and perception of our life and calling together. Prayer shapes the church to see her highest calling. Prayer is about and for God. Prayer calls us not to try and reach the heavens with our own abilities and somehow try and establish our own godless kingdom, but to surrender ourselves and all that we bring to God, and to see him as the source and total of all that we are. Prayer, therefore, is not a means to an end, a vending machine spirituality, but communion with Father, Son, and Spirit, time to be shaped and molded by the Spirit ever more into the image of Christ. This is the ongoing work of God by his Spirit who, "through His transcendent love, became what we are, that he might bring us to be even what he is himself."[10]

The place of contemplation was significant for Jesus in his own ministry. Mark's gospel records that "while it was still very dark, Jesus got up and went out to a deserted place, and there he prayed." (Mark 1:35) It is important that we see taking ourselves off to quiet places and praying as an integral part of our lives and not simply a yearly thing that happens on retreat. The desert fathers and mothers were only too aware of the need to pray, to find space for divine opportunity, and to seek God in the desert of our own hearts. Prayer in the all and everything meant a slow and gentle shaping of the Spirit. They believed that God would use our prayers to shape us "little by little" until we eventually become what we are "meant to become."[11] This is why prayer is vital to the discovery of our humanity and the battle against dehumanization. In a time when how busy and effective

9. Bonhoeffer, *The Cost of Discipleship*, 163.

10. Irenaeus, *Against Heresies*, V. Preface.

11. Williams, *Silence and Honey Cakes*, 87.

you are is the measure of your humanity, stillness, meditation, and prayer can be seen as a waste of time and a distraction to what it important.

This commitment to prayer, to contemplation and a way of prayerfulness, is therefore incredibly difficult in this world of speed, violence, and constant activity, where success and usefulness is measured by "growth." Ministers especially have a difficult task to stay true to a life of prayer, recognizing themselves that prayer truly is the first and best thing that they should be engaged in. The temptation is to see your worth and usefulness according to how big your church is and how busy you are. As a minister I am all too aware of these thoughts and temptations, and so keeping prayer as foundational and first in my own ministry is difficult at times. Yet I am convinced that prayer is without doubt the very best and first calling of a minister and all who are called to follow Jesus. When churches begin to seek a minister who is more like a CEO, then we can be sure the dehumanization and secularization of church has firmly taken hold. Within my own ministry I am regularly seeing various people from all walks of life, with all kinds of circumstances and situations being played out. The very best thing I can do for each of them is pray. But more than that, if I am not a person of prayer, then I will not be the person and presence I need to be for them. Ministry is about the care of souls; therefore, the minister's soul needs daily renewal through the Spirit by a spirit of prayerfulness. This is where the Psalms are so incredibly important.

THE PSALMS AND PRAYER

For Bonhoeffer, like Luther before him,[12] the Psalms are the great prayer book of the church. "From ancient times in the church a special significance has been placed on the praying of the psalms together . . . we now must recover the meaning of praying the psalms."[13] It was the praying of the Psalms that sustained him throughout his time in prison at the hands of the Nazi regime. In a letter to his parents he writes, "I read the Psalms every day, as I have done for years; I know them and love them more than

---

12. "The Christian can learn to pray in the psalter, for here he can hear how the saints talk with God. The number of moods which are expressed here, joy and suffering, hope and care, make it possible for every Christian to find himself in it, and to pray with the psalms." Pelikan, "Preface to the Psalter," 254.

13. Bonhoeffer, *Life Together,* 53.

any other book."[14] For Bonhoeffer the Psalms were not only something to be prayed individually as a means through which we were drawn closer to God, but they were also the prayer book of the church that the church were called to pray together. Bonhoeffer said that "[t]he only way to understand the Psalms is on your knees, the whole congregation praying the words of the Psalms with all its strength."[15] Bonhoeffer understood well the significance and need of the Psalms to the life and health of those called to ministry, having experienced firsthand the desert of trial and temptation. Some people earn the right to demand greater holiness, more faithful discipleship, and passion for prayer from those called into ministry and the church, and Bonhoeffer is one such person. The honesty and challenge of the Psalms enable the minister and consequently the church to resist notions of sentimentality and go deeper into truthful worship of the living God. André Chouraqui declares that when we read the Psalms we become

> . . . identified with the one . . . who groans and who suffers, who undergoes the assault of iniquity, and who bleeds and who is put to death, and yet never stops singing the utterly fantastic certitude which inundates him. The soul is carried away by the incantations of the Hebraic rhythms; and slowly, very slowly, the soul of the psalmist becomes our soul; his combat becomes our combat; his pain our pain; his agony our agony—the agony of all who, throughout age after age, have committed their life to this living flame. Slowly, very slowly, the soul becomes penetrated by, and nourished by, the eternal soul of the sweet singer of Israel. The burst of light which overwhelms him transpierces us; the light he seeks dazzles us, and transforms our darkness into ineffable joy."[16]

Therefore, with Chouraqui, Bonhoeffer, and Luther, we should make the Psalms our own daily prayers[17] as well as a weekly feature of the life of the church we have been called to. The Psalms, as Chouraqui so elegantly points out, reveal our humanity, and so prayer must enable us to embrace the truthfulness of our condition and situation. With triumphalism and "fix you" models of prayer, we lose our humanity to idealism and insanity, whereas honest prayer, such as we see in the Psalms, is an embrace of real-

---

14. Bonhoeffer, *Meditations on the Psalms*, 113–4.

15. Ibid, 11.

16. Choraqui, "The Psalms," 30–1.

17. I pray Psalm 51 every day: "Have mercy on me, O God, according to your unfailing love."

ity, a journey into the very depths of God's life, and so a discovery of our true humanity.

Prayer as an entry into the Trinitarian life is not something *I do* but that which the Holy Spirit does *for me*. In a surrender of my own desire and agenda, I come to recognize God's prior work in my life calling me to this place of prayer and relationship. It is always the Holy Spirit calling me to the depths of God's "infinite tenderness"; but it is also the Holy Spirit who first painfully darkens my prior certainties, checks my own desires, and so invites me ever more deeply into the life of redemption in Christ.[18] This is what Paul is speaking of in Romans 8, for it is the Holy Spirit who

> . . . helps us in our weakness; for we do not know how to pray as we ought, but that very Spirit intercedes with sighs too deep for words. And God, who searches the heart, knows what is the mind of the Spirit, because the Spirit intercedes for the saints according to the will of God.[19]

This same Spirit is the One through whom we mysteriously and wonderfully are able to call God "Abba! Father," and so bear witness that we are children of God (Romans 8:14–17). John of the Cross describes it beautifully when he explores the tender beckoning of the Spirit upon our soul, declaring that he "raises the soul most sublimely with that his divine breath . . . that she may breathe in God the same breath of love that the Father breathes in the Son and the Son in the Father."[20] To pray, then, is to be invited into the divine dance of God, to be shaped and molded by the Spirit to become more fully human, more like Christ, and thus to see the world in a kaleidoscope of color: broken yet beautiful, groaning yet being renewed, painful and joyful. To pray is to see the world and to respond to the world, not be carried off into some kind of spiritual otherworldliness but to incarnate ourselves in reality of the world around us.

DOMINATION AND POWER

This then will bring us into direct conflict with the "Principalities and Powers" of this world, powers that seek to put themselves in the place of God and change people into their dehumanizing likeness. "For our struggle is

18. Coakley, *God, Sexuality, and the Self*, 56.

19. Rom 8:26–27.

20. John of the Cross, *Spiritual Canticle*, 39.3.

not against enemies of blood and flesh, but against the rulers, against the authorities, against the cosmic powers of this present darkness, against the spiritual forces of evil in the heavenly places."[21] Prayer calls us to be human and be changed into the likeness of Christ. When we allow violence and hatred to consume us, our hearts dry up and we are changed ever more into the likeness of the Beastly Systems and Powers that demand our worship and loyalty yet will only lead to our destruction.[22] Prayer is not simply the personal engagement with God, it is also the struggle "to be human in the face of suprahuman Powers."[23] It is a direct assault on the Powers as we pray for the Kingdom of God and for the will of God to be manifest in the structures and Systems of this world. To pray, then, is

> . . . to build your own house. To pray is to discover that Someone else is within your house. To pray is to recognize that it is not your house at all. To keep praying is to have no house to protect because there is only One House. And that One House is everybody's Home. . . . That is the politics of prayer. And that is probably why truly spiritual people are always a threat to politicians of any sort. They want our allegiance and we can no longer give it. Our house is too big.[24]

Prayer reorients us to the Divine Life, calling us to unmask the Powers that enslave and dehumanize. Prayer is a hospital for our own corrupted spiritual lives. Prayer is to see each person through the lens of Triune love and so share our life with them as God has already shared his love and his life with us. Prayer is not a vending machine spirituality as though you put a prayer in and God gives you something back; rather, it is an invitation into the life of God, yet such an invitation does not mean you will not find yourself in the wilderness or in times of doubt or uncertainty of God's very existence. It may even be that, for us to discover an ever more Christlike humanity, we may be driven into the desert of unbelief to meet with God in ever more intimate ways, and it is here that we continue.

---

21. Eph 6:12.

22. Walter Wink does a masterly work of unmasking the "Principalities and Powers" interpreting and making sense of Revelation 12 and 13 in a chapter of his book *Engaging the Powers*. The Beast and the Dragon in Revelation are, according to Wink, a "monstrous spirit" with power and authority upon the earth leading people to violence and destruction. See Chapter Five, "Unmasking the Domination System," 87–104.

23. Wink, *Engaging the Powers*, 297.

24. Rohr, "Prayer as a Political Activity," quoted in Wink, *Engaging the Powers*, 306.

Chapter 9

Trauma

"I dreamed of you," she said in a soft, wondering voice.

"I dreamed you were wandering in the dark, and so was I. We found each other."

John Coffey said nothing. "We found each other in the dark," she said.'

MELLY MOORES, *THE GREEN MILE*

"At three o'clock Jesus cried out with a loud voice, 'Eloi, Eloi, lema sabachthani?' which means 'My God, my God, why have you forsaken me?'"[1]

This is perhaps *the* greatest atheistic cry in all of history. Here, as the Son of God hangs on the splintered wood of the Cross, a cry echoes out into the desolation and the darkness, a cry of felt abandonment, a cry of suffering, a cry of despair. John Colwell in *Why Have You Forsaken Me?* highlights how there have been various ways of reading this cry of forsakenness throughout church history, attempts to lessen the horror or qualify the cry.[2] He argues that a common attempt at this is to assume that Jesus is deliberately quoting the first lines of Psalm 22 as a means of drawing listeners to the hopeful end of that Psalm, thus subverting the horror of the crucifixion and in fact declaring his ultimate victory and resurrection. Read

1. Mark 15:33–34.
2. See Colwell, *Why Have You Forsaken Me?*, 77–91.

Psalm 22 and notice how throughout the psalm we move from forsaken-ness to triumph, from despair to hope:

> My God, my God, why have you forsaken me?
>> Why are you so far from helping me, from the words of my groaning?
> O my God, I cry by day, but you do not answer;
>> and by night, but find no rest . . .
> Yet it was you who took me from the womb;
>> you kept me safe on my mother's breast.
> On you I was cast from my birth,
>> and since my mother bore me you have been my God . . .
>
> I am poured out like water,
>> and all my bones are out of joint;
> my heart is like wax;
>> it is melted within my breast;
> my mouth is dried up like a potsherd,
>> and my tongue sticks to my jaws;
>> you lay me in the dust of death . . .
> But you, O Lord, do not be far away!
>> O my help, come quickly to my aid!
> Deliver my soul from the sword,
>> my life from the power of the dog!
>> Save me from the mouth of the lion! . . .
>
> All the ends of the earth shall remember
>> and turn to the Lord;
> and all the families of the nations
>> shall worship before him.
> For dominion belongs to the Lord,
>> and he rules over the nations . . .
> Posterity will serve him;
>> future generations will be told about the Lord,
> and proclaim his deliverance to a people yet unborn,
>> saying that he has done it.

(Ps 22:1–2, 9–10, 14–15, 19–21, 27–28, 30–31)

Another way that this cry has been interpreted is through the lens of all four gospel accounts of the crucifixion. In a similar way to hearing Jesus' cry through the lens of the ultimate triumph of Psalm 22, we hear the cry of Jesus through the lens of the more victorious and triumphant sayings of Jesus on the cross. However, while we undoubtedly want to hear the gospel story in its entirety, we must not lessen the way each of the gospel writers reflects upon the death of Jesus. Colwell highlights how Mark and Matthew record this cry of dereliction with no sense of triumph, no call of forgiveness and committing of his spirit into his Father's hands as in Luke, no "possibly triumphant cry 'It is finished'"[3] as in John, but simply with the reality of darkness, death, and forsakenness. Indeed, Mark's gospel ends with some of the women who followed Jesus going to the tomb, finding it empty, fleeing from it, and not saying anything to anyone because of fear. While there are debates around this ending and whether a fuller and extended ending should be considered,[4] we must not exclude the possibility that Mark wanted to end his gospel in this abrupt manner for theological reasons. Maybe he wanted his readers to encounter the trauma and uncertainty of the event of the crucifixion? Another method has been to emphasize that while Jesus is truly and fully human, he is also truly and fully God, and God is beyond suffering, thus leaving us with a cry that is not as desperate as we might have previously thought. Without getting into a whole debate on divine impassibility,[5] what this position effectively does is to deny the reality of Christ's humanity in all its fullness[6] as well as to make "breathtaking assumptions about . . . who God is, about what God can and cannot do,"[7] and about how God has revealed himself throughout human history.

It is not surprising that theologians within Christian history have attempted to soften then the weight of the cry of despair, yet in doing so we may well miss the significance of the cry for our own humanity and faith. As a cry it leaves us with doubt and uncertainty, yet these are those things that actually enable us to become more fully human, that counter the

---

3. Ibid, 82.

4. For instance see Lunn, *The Original Ending of Mark*.

5. Divine impassibility is the doctrine that God cannot suffer.

6. "This assumed and confessed divine impassibility led all too easily in the Early Church to the mirror imaged denials that are docetism (God does not suffer therefore Jesus only seemed to be truly human and only seemed to suffer) and adoptionism (God does not suffer therefore Jesus, as one who is truly human and truly suffers, cannot be truly God)." Colwell, *Why Have You Forsaken Me?*, 84.

7. Ibid.

dehumanization of certainty and sameness. Let me unpack these ideas of "certainty" and "sameness" a little more.

CERTAINTY AND SAMENESS

There is a real danger within all of us to simply construct our beliefs and desires based upon the beliefs and desires of another person. So we end up with relationships that confer upon ourselves a "sense of sameness," relationships that are, in the words of Lacan, "narcissistic embraces."[8] Marcus Pound argues that this is a far easier thing to do, to incorporate the desires and certainties of another, because it means that we do not have to confront the lack, the uncertainty, the doubt that resides within each of us.[9] What Lacan called our "desire of the Other"[10] and René Girard calls *mimesis* is seen powerfully in the narrative preceding the crucifixion of Jesus.

It is close to the time that Jesus will be arrested and condemned to die, and the tension around his teaching and presence is continuing to grow. We encounter a scene in the gospels of Jesus riding into Jerusalem on the colt of a donkey, an echo to the ancient prophecy that declared,

> Rejoice greatly, O daughter Zion!
> > Shout aloud, O daughter Jerusalem!
> Lo, your king comes to you;
> > Triumphant and victorious is he,
> Humble and riding on a donkey,
> > On a colt, the foal of a donkey.[11]

This action of Jesus was surely a highly charged political and religious act, as many people laid their cloaks on the ground singing and celebrating Jesus' arrival as God's promised Messiah, the Deliver, Vindicator, and King who would bring freedom and deliverance to the people of God. A few days later, however, we encounter another scene with the crowds, this time no longer singing and shouting praise to Jesus—we hear them shouting "Crucify him!" Rather than this merely being about "mob mentality," we see whole groups of people taking upon themselves the *certainty* that is

8. Lacan, *Écrits*, 249.

9. Pound, *Theology, Psychoanalysis and Trauma*, 120.

10. Lacan, *The Seminar of Jacques Lacan XI*, 235.

11. Zech 9:9.

given to them through a particular system of belief. Jesus is seemingly the One who offers the people a sense of sameness, belief, and desire that they are looking for through his arrival into Jerusalem on a donkey, yet when they see him standing before them beaten and bloodied, they no longer believe that this Jesus could possibly offer the certainty that they previously had desired. By projecting onto Jesus through his trial and death their own fear of doubt, lack, and uncertainty, expressed through violence, they once again regain a sense of certainty, and order is restored. Yet in the death of Jesus nothing is the same again. Let us interpret the death of Jesus through the idea of magic and illusions and consider how his death and the trauma of his death might enable us to become more fully human.

THE MAGIC OF THE CROSS

Magic calls us to suspend our disbelief, and in many ways religion also calls us to enter a world where we are invited to believe the unbelievable. A film that is helpful for us here is *The Prestige* by Christopher Nolan, starring Christian Bale and Hugh Jackman. The film revolves around two magicians, Angier (Jackman) and Borden (Bale), who are fierce rivals and desire to create the perfect illusion that will captivate the crowds. Near the beginning of the film we are told what a magician does in a trick,

> Every great magic trick consists of three parts or acts. The first part is called "The Pledge." The magician shows you something ordinary: a deck of cards, a bird, or a man. He shows you this object. Perhaps he asks you to inspect it to see if it is indeed real, unaltered, normal. But of course, it probably isn't. The second act is called "The Turn." The magician takes the ordinary something and makes it do something extraordinary. Now you're looking for the secret, but you won't find it, because of course you're not really looking. You don't really want to know. You want to be fooled. But you wouldn't clap yet. Because making something disappear isn't enough; you have to bring it back. That's why every magic trick has a third act, the hardest part, the part we call "The Prestige."

With the death of Jesus we are invited into The Prestige.[12] The first part, "The Pledge," is Jesus' triumphant ride into Jerusalem. As we have already seen,

---

12. Others have used *The Prestige* in theology, so what I write here is not unique in the sense of originality, but unique in my own adaptation and interpretation. For more see Rollins, *The Divine Magician*, and Brewin, *After Magic*.

Jesus is welcomed into the city with joy and celebration, expectation and hope. The people are waiting for him to be their long-awaited Messiah, the one promised by God in ancient times to free them from tyranny, expose the gods of their oppressors as false, and establish the reign of God through his messianic actions, actions that we assume will be violent and warrior-like, for that surely is the only way God deals with tyrants and oppressors? Is not violence the only way God establishes his Kingdom on earth? So we have the anticipation of "The Pledge," and all of us wait expectantly for the act to unfold. Next is "The Turn." Jesus is arrested. This is not how things were supposed to go. The Messiah does not get arrested and charged with blasphemy. The Messiah is not supposed to be taken before Pilate and subjected to mockery and humiliation. Has something gone wrong? Perhaps, however, this is a part of the trick, and so we continue to watch, waiting once again, expectantly, suspending our disbelief for the grand finale of "The Prestige," the point where we clap and cheer and walk away discussing and wondering how he did it. Yet what do we see? The so-called Messiah hanging beaten, bloodied, and naked on a cross.

Is that it? Is this what we have been waiting for? A dead man? Like the rest of the crowd, we walk away in dismay, our belief in the unbelievable suspended, perhaps even discarded for good.

But this is actually "The Prestige," the defining moment of the act, the hardest part, the third act, the moment of brilliance and transformation, for God is dead, and no one saw that coming:

> We proclaim Christ crucified, a stumbling block to Jews and foolishness to Gentiles. 1 Cor 1:23

There is a tendency for us to not quite believe that at the death of Jesus God actually dies. Now we use the language of death, we thank God for giving us his Son over to death so that we might live, yet something within us, if we are truthful to ourselves, does not quite believe that Jesus actually died in the same way loved ones die. We know he died and was buried, yet, in words we cannot quite express, we do not ascribe to Jesus the totality of death because, well, it is Jesus! This most often finds expression through our inability in most evangelical churches to "do" Good Friday. Such is our obvious discomfort with the concept of the death of God that the Good Friday service often ends up with an "It's OK, Sunday's coming" clause to highlight that Jesus did not stay dead— resurrection is on its way. But if we are to hear the Gospel story properly, if our desire is for the Holy Spirit to shape us according to this story, then we need to stay in the moment when God dies and not rush ahead to resurrection. The death of the Son of God is not only the defining moment for all Christians everywhere; it is the defining moment for all of creation "when, after having reunited all things in Christ, God will become all in all.'[13] Here death unleashes its worst upon the One who is Life, and the One who is Life dies. He dies. The Son of God dies. God is dead.

GOOD FRIDAY

Within my own ministry I have for some time now sought to encourage Jesus followers to stay at Good Friday and not rush ahead to Easter Sunday. So at Good Friday services we used Mark's gospel to be our story, to allow this version of events to be our version of events and so, as far as possible, to hear the cry of forsakenness as a cry without answer—so that when we go to bed that Good Friday evening, Jesus is dead.

To highlight what I am talking about, here is a sermon I wrote for Good Friday one year. As you read it, I encourage you to stay in this scene of crucifixion and allow yourself to be shaped by this scene.

> Mark 15:33–39
>
> *At the sixth hour darkness came over the whole land until the ninth hour. And at the ninth hour Jesus cried out in a loud voice, "Eloi, Eloi, lama sabachthani?"—which means, "My God, my God, why have you forsaken me?" When some of those standing near heard this, they said, "Listen, he's calling Elijah." One man ran, filled a sponge with wine vinegar, put it on a stick, and offered it to Jesus to drink. "Now leave him alone. Let's see if Elijah comes to take him down," he said. With a loud cry, Jesus breathed his last. The curtain of the temple was torn in two from top to bottom. And when the centurion, who stood there in front of Jesus, heard his cry and saw how he died, he said, "Surely this man was the Son of God!"*
>
> Stand with me at the scene of the cross. Here there is no Easter Sunday, no glorious resurrection. No, the cross is what we are faced with. Right here, right now, the cross is our reality. Right here at the cross, right now at the cross, this is all we know.
>
> We have walked with Jesus as he taught with authority and wisdom. We have marveled with the crowds as he healed the sick and raised the dead. We have celebrated with singing as this young

---

13. Lossky, *In the Image and Likeness of God*, 110.

Galilean rode into Jerusalem on the colt of a donkey, seemingly the Messiah we had all been waiting for. Yet now we stand in the darkness of this scene of crucifixion, and all that has gone before seems distant, irrelevant and worthless. For before our eyes hangs this man, this same man.

How do you respond to the man on the cross?

Darkness envelops the land, and now, as our eyes squint and strain through the shadows, we feel relieved because we cannot see as clearly the fullness of the horror of the scene. The blackness now seems to hide it. But then what our eyes miss our ears do not, and a gut-wrenching sound echoes out in the midst of the darkness.

"My God, my God, why have you forsaken me?"

Here, at this sound, the darkness of the land cannot hide the reality of the scene before us. Here, at this sound, our ears do not need to strain to know what is happening, for here, at this sound, we glimpse the truth of the horror of the event; this God-Man feels god-forsaken.

His cry comes from the depths of his heart, for here he feels alone, here he feels abandoned. He is not singing a Psalm to prove his messiahship (Psalm 22). He is in torment, a place of unimaginable pain. Surely for Jesus the darkness is accompanied by felt silence. Here as he hangs on the cross, Jesus can no longer hear his Father's voice, as he did at his baptism, calling him the delight of his life (Mark 1:11).

But before we turn away from this scene in some attempt to remove ourselves from it, look once again at Jesus. As Jesus hangs in darkness and despair are we not confronted with the reality of *our* situation? For should it not be us who hang there in darkness and despair because of the enormity of our sin? Because we have not loved God with all our heart soul, mind, and strength, because we have not loved one another with all that we are, the One that has, hangs in our place. As he is suspended in our place, we see and hear the horror of our sin and its consequences. Our violence unleashes its worst upon the Son of God, and willingly he endures its brutality.

As Jesus hangs on the cross, the powers of sin, death, violence, and darkness unleash their horror upon him—powers that we were meant to feel the weight of. Yet in darkness and despair, Jesus experiences the weight of sin so we do not have to. Jesus hangs there so that we can be reconciled to God and to each other, so that *we* do not have to cry out, "My God, my God, why have you forsaken me?"—for how could we ask such a question when we face the actuality of our sin? In that he takes our place, it has been decided what our place is.

How then do you respond to the man on the cross?

As we hear the depths of despair in the voice of the Son of God, how do we respond? Do we stand and discuss together what his cry might mean, cold to the reality of the suffering he endures? Or do we leave the group for a second and present Jesus a token offering on the end of a stick, as though this weak gesture might soften the weight of cross that hangs on his back?

How do you respond to the man on the cross?

As Jesus hangs in darkness, do we concede that it has overcome him (John 1:5)? Has the Light of the World been extinguished for good?

When glimpsing the horror of the scene, hearing the depth of the despair, and as we hear Jesus cry out and see the way he died, do we, with the centurion, say, "Surely this man was the Son of God"?

But do not merely gaze at the scene as if staring at the scene itself is enough. No, be sure that here God has done something, God has taken the first step, God, in his grace, has made it possible for us to respond. A mystery has occurred here at the cross, a mystery that we are invited to share in. Here in such starkness and brutality, God reveals himself to us that we might respond to him.

But how will you respond? Will you leave here today and continue in your life as though the death of Jesus has nothing to do with you? Will you call judgment down on others, unaware that we are all equals at this scene of crucifixion? Or will you accept that your identity is shaped and defined by this Jesus who hangs on the cross? Because God has suffered here on the cross, you too are called to embrace your identity, which is defined by the crucified Son of God. Will you today commit your life afresh to God and allow God's Spirit to transform you more into the person he wants you to be? And will you go from here that others may see and hear the crucified Jesus through you?

How then will you respond to the man on the cross?

To indwell this scene is to take seriously the trauma of the scene. A sermon like this is intended to be a means through which we recognize the reality of the death of Jesus without rushing ahead to resurrection. Here we are confronted with death. It is common for us in Western society to be death-deniers and so search for ways to lessen the impact and truthfulness of death.

DEATH DENIERS

In *The City of God,* Augustine believed that the Roman elites indulged in all kinds of questionable practices to blunt the fear of death that hung over them. Augustine argued that "the essential context for ambition is a people corrupted by greed and sensuality."[14] The fear of death, argued Augustine, accompanied by fear of loss of status and power, caused the Roman elite to seek ways to make the memory of themselves last forever; and the main way was through war. So a continued desire for power, status, and wealth consumed the Roman Empire, and such desire seems to be replicated in our modern societies, epitomized by our avarice. What this greed does to us is to search for security, as though security will not only protect our lives but will also protect our "stuff." Such is our aversion to death that security seems to be a god deserving worship, a god that we desperately are seeking to please. On the idolatry of security, Bonhoeffer says,

> How does peace come about? Through a system of political trea-
> ties? Through the investment of international capital in different
> countries? Through the big banks, through money? Or through
> universal peaceful rearmament to guarantee peace? Through none
> of these, for the single reason of them all: peace is confused with
> safety. There is no way to peace along the way of safety. For peace
> must be dared. It is the great venture. It can never be safe. Peace is
> the opposite of security. To demand guarantees is to mistrust, and
> this mistrust in turn brings forth war.

This demand for security leaves no place for doubt. Certainty is demanded in order that our fear of death is abated. Like the Romans before us, we desire ways to make the memory of ourselves live forever and so somehow eradicate the reality of our death. Yet we need to be woken up out of our death-denying slumber and embrace the reality of the trauma of death. The death of Jesus enables us to do just this—but not only this, it enables us to discover the truthfulness of our humanity in light of our own doubt epito-mized by Jesus' cry of forsakenness on the cross.

Slavoj Žižek argues that the book of Job highlights how our suffering is meaningless and therefore is the first step to delegitimizing suffering. Christianity, therefore, according to Žižek, is the outworking of this real-ity, that suffering is meaningless. For Žižek the death of Jesus resolves the

---

14. Augustine, *City of God,* 42.1.31

problems of "the abyss of the Other's desire." In other words, we do not know what God wants from us, and that is OK—or as Lacan puts it,

"Che vuoi?"[15]

What dies then is the guarantee of the big Other. The big Other (French: "L'Autre") is Lacan's concept for that place—be it science, an ideology, God, reason—where I believe the truth about my existence and who I am, the meaning of my life, my identity, to be located; who I am is found in this "thing."

In psychoanalysis, a person exists through a lack, a split, a fissure. We may have dreams of being complete, and perhaps at a very early point in our lives we felt no lack, no split, no separation, being just one with whatever surrounded us. But as far as we are creatures of language and desire (and to Lacan language and desire are what separate the human from the animal being), we are split beings: split between "things" and "words," between what we want and what we get, between what we feel like and what we look like, between present and past, between what we think we say or want and what we actually say or want (that is, between conscious and unconscious). In Jesus' cry of forsakenness we discover the One who has experienced total lack, a cry of felt abandonment, where that total sense of Oneness with his Father is questioned. In this felt sense of lack and split, Jesus fully identifies with humanity, being able to "free those who all their lives were held in slavery to the fear of death." (Heb 2:15) In Jesus, humanity has One who is able "to sympathize with our weaknesses . . . one who in every respect has been tested as we are. . . . " (Heb 4:15) So the message of Christianity is radically atheistic according to Žižek, because here we witness the death of the god who guarantees meaning to our suffering.[16] That is not to say that he believes life is meaningless, but that is to say that his atheism does not seek to fill the void left by the death of God with some other big Other. This is where he radically differs from the New Atheists who would like to eradicate all religion from the public sphere and fill it instead with another form of faith according to atheistic creeds. In the death of Jesus, then, we hear his cry of forsakenness, and we are confronted with the ultimate traumatic event: the One who is truly human suffers the fullness of sin and violence and death upon him. Therefore, in our own doubt and

15. "What do you want from me?"

16. See https://www.youtube.com/watch?v=tABnznhzdIY from *A Pervert's Guide to Ideology*

uncertainty, we are invited into this traumatic event for ourselves, invited into the abyss of unknowingness and the darkness of the cross. Here in our doubt and uncertainty we are not seeking meaning but rather the honest words to pray that God may be invited into our doubt and uncertainty, into our everyday. The trauma of the cross "destabilizes meaning"[17] and allows for new possibilities in our faith to be opened up. In psychoanalytic terms, trauma is the only "real" event. Throughout our lives we give meaning to every event and moment, interpreting them according to our own preconceived ideas of reality. For instance, when we see a shooting star, we are seeing something Imaginary and Symbolic; our vision occurs through a whole series of events that enable us to see: light reflecting, preconceived ideas of a shooting star, distance from the object, reception of the image. All of this makes sight possible. Trauma, or the Real, is something that happens before we have an opportunity to interpret what is happening; we are simply confronted with what "is" and have to live in the reality of "is"; unexpected joy, pain, or fear are Real. Now we may add meaning and interpret these events later, but in the moment, "is" is Real.

The Cross of Jesus is *the* "is" moment.

In other words, God dies—and we have no idea what that means.

"The Prestige" of the cross is something completely unexpected, destabilizing, and scandalous, "a stumbling block" and "foolishness," as Paul puts it.[18] He goes on reminding the church in Corinth that in the call to preach Christ crucified God chose, by the standards of a world of certainty and strength, people who were foolish, weak, the low, the despised, and people regarded as nothing, so that no one could boast in God's presence or even about God's presence. Paul vowed to preach nothing but Christ and him crucified in order to demonstrate, though the Holy Spirit, the power of God;[19] the power of God is seen through the trauma of the crucifix-

17. Pound, *Theology, Psychoanalysis and Trauma*, 22.

18. 1 Cor 1:23.

19. "Consider your own call, brothers and sisters: not many of you were wise by human standards, not many were powerful, not many were of noble birth. But God chose what is foolish in the world to shame the wise; God chose what is weak in the world to shame the strong; God chose what is low and despised in the world, things that are not, to reduce to nothing things that are, so that no one might boast in the presence of God. He is the source of your life in Christ Jesus, who became for us wisdom from God, and righteousness and sanctification and redemption, in order that, as it is written, 'Let the one who boasts, boast in the Lord.' When I came to you, brothers and sisters, I did not come proclaiming the mystery of God to you in lofty words or wisdom. For I decided to know nothing among you except Jesus Christ, and him crucified. And I came to you

ion. Here we see why Žižek's insights are so helpful. God is not the big Other who gives meaning to our suffering or the promise of overcoming our suffering that is sometimes offered through science or consumerism or religion. Rather, in the death of God we discover a God embracing us in the darkness, death, and filth, never promising us a life free from trauma, but promising to be with us through it. This is the God who says "I am with you," "Never will I leave you." This is why the regular commitment to sharing in the Lord's Supper is vital to the sustaining of Christian communities.

THE MEAL

Here in this sacrament God meets with us and in his grace, by his Spirit, enables Jesus' story to become our story.

> The ultimate goal of the Supper is our participation in Christ and our transformation through that participation—and that participation and transformation occurs through the entirety of our sacramental indwelling of Christ, through our indwelling of the gospel story, and through the mediating presence and action of the Spirit.[20]

Aside from the often sentimental and nostalgic notions of mere remembrance often associated with the Lord's Supper in contemporary evangelical, charismatic churches, it is the denial of the promise of God's presence and the undermining of Christ's transforming power through this meal that is so troubling. It is a further example of our inability to indwell the trauma and uncertainty of the cross and allow it to shape our identity and faith. Here at this meal, God is present in a unique and significant way. As we break the bread and share the cup, God meets with us, and we, in a mysterious way, are opened up once again to this Christ event that, although it occurred 2000 years ago, reaches through time and space, bringing about a transformation of the whole cosmos. Each time we share this meal, we stand at the darkness of the crucifixion and hear the atheistic cry of forsakenness and know that in the hearing of that cry our faith can be rooted in doubt and uncertainty. The trauma of this meal is vital for the church.

---

in weakness and in fear and in much trembling. My speech and my proclamation were not with plausible words of wisdom, but with a demonstration of the Spirit and of power, so that your faith might rest not on human wisdom but on the power of God." 1 Cor 1:26—2:5.

20. Colwell, *Promise and Presence*, 175.

Here then, is the paradoxical beauty of the Lord's Supper. As we take and eat the body of Christ, take and drink the blood of Christ, we are invited into the place of doubt and uncertainty, and yet in this place God is present. His Spirit is with us, and so even in a place of our total rejection of God or our felt absence of God, he is with us. The curtain of the temple has been torn in two, meaning that God is with us, no longer hidden behind the vicissitudes of the powerful, but present everywhere, especially among the weak and those regarded as nothing. The Cross is the ultimate symbol of the rejected, the forsaken, the cursed, and the despised, yet at the Cross God is most present. At the cross we see our rejection of God, our violence, and our disorientating sinfulness crucified so that God can woo us back to himself, vowing to draw all people to himself through his effervescent love, compassion, and grace. God is always the One who takes the first step towards us, the One who runs to us, the One who "while we are still sinners" dies for us. God does not need the cross to forgive us,[21] God is not using the cross to placate his anger like a mythological monster; rather, through the cross God deals with *our* wrath—the New Testament says we are children of wrath[22]—deals with our violence, and deals with the totality of death that our sinfulness enslaves us to. Our sin distorts and disorients us away from God and his divine life, yet in Christ we are reoriented back towards God through the narrow gate that can only be discovered when we are not staggering around intoxicated by our sin. In this sacramental meal, we encounter God and are invited to walk the treacherous road to peace, and in doing so to shake off the dehumanizing ways that certainty enslaves us to and discover freedom in a God who embraces us in all our doubt.

---

21. "Had it been a case of a trespass only, and not of a subsequent corruption, repentance would have been well enough; but when once transgression had begun, men came under the power of the corruption proper to their nature and were bereft of the grace which belonged to them as creatures in the Image of God. No, repentance could not meet the case. What—or rather Who was it that was needed for such grace and such recall as we required? Who, save the Word of God Himself, Who also in the beginning had made all things out of nothing? His part it was, and His alone, both to bring again the corruptible to incorruption and to maintain for the Father His consistency of character with all." Athanasius, *On the Incarnation*, 2.7.

22. Eph 2:3.

Chapter 10

Sex

We've always defined ourselves by our ability to overcome the impossible. And we count these moments. These moments that we dare to aim higher, to break barriers, to reach for the stars, to make the unknown known. We count these moments as our proudest achievements. But we lost all that. Or perhaps we've just forgotten that we are still pioneers. And we've barely begun. And that our greatest accomplishments cannot be behind us, because our destiny lies above us.

COOPER, *INTERSTELLAR*

M aximus the Confessor describes how the natural will of humanity is always "bent" towards the Good, that ultimately our desire is for God, even if that desire is towards godlessness. He says, "No creature has ever ceased using the inherent power that directs it towards its end, nor has it ceased the natural activity that impels it towards its end."[1] In other words, God is the ground and end of all desire because God is the Ultimate Good, the end. This does not mean that sinful desire is from God, but that sinful desire is misplaced desire, disoriented as we are by sin, trying to stagger towards God without even knowing it but often getting lost on the way.

God is not another object in the world of consumerism or market-place of impulse and preference; rather, God is the "good end" which all things seek. It is easy to continue to view God as another "thing among things" or "object among objects," as Tillich revealed to us earlier, but God

1. Maximus the Confessor, *Ambiguum 7*, 50.

quite simply is not like this. You cannot choose or reject God as you can the latest Apple watch or a pair of jeans, for God is not a finite object; God is "all in all," and so cannot be turned away from like you would anything else. God is the fount, source and goal of all things, "things visible and invisible, whether thrones or dominions or rulers or powers—all things have been created through him and for him."[2] Human desire, then, finds itself defined in and through God. Misplaced desire that is not founded in Ultimate Good will undoubtedly lead us toward that which strips of us our true humanity, robbing us of our ability to be a people of creative acts of love that point to life with God. Right sexual desire, then, finds its origins in divine desire, the human will seeking God and being conformed ever more into the likeness of Christ, which is the ultimate *telos* of all people. Therefore sex is about God rather "God" being about sex as Freud defined it.[3]

YOU SEXY THING

Sex saturates our culture, so much so that we are often oblivious to the impact and degree to which it is used to influence us. Advertisers rely on sex selling and so use it to appeal to our superficial desires in the hope that we will not only be drawn to their waters but that we will take a long drink from the fountain of consumerism. We are bombarded regularly by the images of the "perfect" person, glimmering in the sunshine, a life without pain or sorrow, attached to the latest product the company is selling. Time and again the sexual attractiveness of the people within the ad is emphasized, somehow telling us that through this product we could be like them. Mimetic desire is crucial for advertisers; we begin by wanting the product because we want to be the person we see with the product.

Sex is a powerful tool to lure us in for advertisers, but more than this, it is a powerful tool for capitalism, which is why pornography is so effective in a capitalist society. Capitalism is an economic system that operates through the production of wealth, the creation of "more," and gives legitimacy to our greed. While politicians keep telling us that the only way to

---

2. Col 1:16b.

3. Freud believed that all religious belief was an illusion, a desire to deal with guilt that has sprung from sexual repression as a child. Freud believed "that at the bottom of every case of hysteria there are one or more occurrences of premature sexual experience, occurrences which belong to the earliest years of childhood . . . " Masson, *The Assault on Truth*, 263.

save the nation is by spending our money, then we can regularly justify our greed, not only to ourselves but also to those who suffer directly as a result of our greed and selfishness. As Alasdair MacIntyre points out,

> Christianity has to view any social and economic order that treats being or becoming rich as highly desirable as doing wrong to those who must not only accept its goals, but succeed in achieving them. Riches are, from a biblical point of view, an affliction, an almost insuperable obstacle to entering the kingdom of heaven. Capitalism is bad for those who succeed by its standards as well as for those who fail by them, something that many preachers and theologians have failed to recognize. And those Christians who have recognized it have often enough been at odds with ecclesiastical as well as political and economic authorities.[4]

Certainly capitalism thrives off of our greed, yet as a system it is more than our greed, "for capitalism . . . cannot be reduced to the egotistic strivings of capitalists for more and more profit."[5] Capitalism, then, takes upon itself a "life" and Power of its own and functions way beyond those who are enslaved to it; it is, as Walter Wink would say, part of a Domination System:

> The Powers are not that system; they are merely the individual institutions and structures deployed under the overall aegis of the Domination System. The Domination System is what obtains when an entire network of Powers becomes hell-bent on control.[6]

Wink is arguing throughout his work on the Powers that there is a Domination System that is rooted in violence and murder, the need for humanity to constantly sacrifice to gods in order to maintain a fragile peace. The System thus takes control,[7] ensuring its survival whatever the cost, ascribing worth according to how much something or someone is valued, that value determined by money and wealth. Without doubt capitalism has made

---

4. MacIntyre, *Marxism and Christianity*, xiv.

5. Žižek, *Living in the End Times*, 131.

6. Wink, *Engaging the Powers*, 49.

7. "Rancière rightly emphasizes the radical ambiguity of the Marxist notion of the gap between formal democracy, with its discourse of the rights of man and political freedom, and the economic reality of exploitation and domination. This gap between the 'appearance' of equality-freedom and the social reality of economic and cultural differences can be interpreted in the standard symptomatic way, namely, that the form of universal rights, equality, freedom and democracy is just a necessary, but illusory, expression of its concrete social content, the universe of exploitation and class domination." Žižek, *Living in the End Times*, 44.

wealth the highest value within our communities and society, a system of economy measured according to its ability to sustain and grow, with profit as the highest social good and the political elite ensuring the propaganda and rhetoric of "those who work hard are rewarded" seeping like poisonous venom into the very bloodstream of modern societal consciousness:

> The Kingdom of Mammon exercises constraint by invisible chains and drives its slaves with invisible prods. (How rare it is for rich people to say, "I have enough.") But Mammon is wiser in its way than the dictator, for money enslaves not by force but by love.[8]

But the control that these things have upon us, the power that Mammon has over us, is more than the things themselves. We find ourselves possessed by our possessions, in love with their existence; but more than this, we are gripped by the *desire* they invoke within us, a desire that springs from mimesis. And this is where pornography and capitalism journey together, for both tap into that basic human mimetic and triangular desire: it is mimetic, for we are imitators; it is triangular in that there is the "model," the "disciple," and the "object" of desire. Let us unpack this idea further.

In both capitalism and pornography we have this triangular event whereby there is us (the disciple), the model or the one who we seek to imitate and be like (the wealthy person or the porn star), and the object of desire (wealth or sexual satisfaction). The nature of pornography is not to make us believe that what we are seeing is "real" in any relational sense, but that it is a fantasy which you are invited in some way to make your own. And this is how capitalism works so well, the invitation into a fantasy that you desire to make your own. Whereas in the past both the ultra-wealthy and hardcore porn were seen as absurd goals for the "common man" through the unrealistic narrative and lives presented to us by porn films and the super-rich, people were suddenly given a chance to pursue these fantasies through the creation of the lottery, celebrity culture, investment opportunities, the internet, and the web-cam. It has meant that people can now pursue the fantasy with a belief it may become reality. The pursuit of unrestrained sexual desire and money inevitably leads to a loss of humanity, a dehumanization of people, as their worth is determined by their value, whether it is sexual or monetary. Certainly there is money to be made within the porn industry, and everybody knows that sex sells, whether through pornography or advertisers. Either way people are made to be an object of desire, owned by capitalism (the model), desired by us (the disciple).

8. Ibid, 50.

DIVINE DESIRE

In the midst of all of this we have to recognize, as Sarah Coakley so beauti-fully puts it, that sexual desire and the desire for God is a "messy entangle-ment." All desire, no matter how godless or wayward, springs forth from a desire for God, a longing for relationship and friendship with the Trinitar-ian Life. Our desires are always a search, a reaching out to become truly human, to know we are loved and have been discovered by our Creator. All too often this "messy entanglement" has resulted in fear on behalf of the church in regard to sex, a fear that will always lead to hate. As Coakley points out, however, there are those within Christian history who have spo-ken in daring ways about sexual desire and desire for God, ways that help us understand human desire better:

> Dionysius with his language of divine desire, Eckhart with his dar-ing sexual metaphors of the birth of Christ in the "virgin" soul, Julian with her "mothering" Christ within the Trinity. All seem to chafe at the edges of acceptable Trinitarian "orthodoxy"; all seek to face or resolve the dilemma of sexual desire and desire for God.[9]

Unhelpfully, sex within church and culture can be seen as the "end game," the goal and purpose of our humanity. Anecdotally, it is always interesting when on a "reality" television program someone in their adulthood admits to being a virgin, and how others always respond to that news at first with a sense of pity, that then turns into being "impressed," that quickly trans-forms into a quest to get that person "laid." Again, anecdotally, during the years I spent drinking heavily and going to nightclubs, the goal was always to find a girl to go home with; sex was the goal.

The challenge Christianity faces today in regard to sex is to not simply make sex the goal too. While pastors and churches would be seeking to en-courage their youngsters to practice abstinence, to wait to have sex until they are married, it seems to me that what they are saying is the same message I would have been telling my friends on a Friday night in a nightclub: the goal is to have sex. We have to be careful that we are not giving out messages to our young people that sex itself, and not marriage, is the actual goal, telling them in unconscious ways that marriage simply legitimizes having sex. We need a healthy view of relationship and a healthy view of sex.

Without doubt we have within us a desire for sex, and the prohibi-tion of sexuality can make sex even more desirable; the more something

9. Coakley, *God, Sexuality and the Self*, 341.

becomes unattainable, the more we desire it. Perhaps this is something of Augustine's problem with lust, for it seems, at least to Augustine, to be something "unnatural," a result of the fall, rather than something that belonged to the nature of humanity before the fall.[10] Yet misplaced desire is not sex. Certainly we can use our sexuality in highly destructive ways, yet sex itself is not the problem. However, once it becomes the "end game," the goal for humanity, then it will become the problem as humanity becomes fixated on one another as purely sexual beings. So when advertisers use sex to sell their products, we find things that usually have no sexual significance become highly sexualized. There is a difference between the goal and the aim of something. Take, for instance, eating, something we do that has a "goal . . . to eliminate hunger, but . . . aim is the satisfaction provided by eating itself."[11] In the masterful program *Hannibal*, Dr. Lecter regularly prepares lavish meals out of/for his guests. There is a theatricality in the experience of dining at the table of Dr. Lecter, for it is more than a meal, it is something to be savored and experienced, an event that plays on all your senses. In one scene Lecter has prepared the cut-off leg of one of his guests who now sits at the table with him.

> Hannibal: Clay roasted side. And canoe-cut marrowbone. I love cooking with clay, it creates a more succulent dish, and adds a little theatricality to dinner. We come from clay, we return to clay. Shall I carve?

> Dr. Gideon: I think you already have. (*Camera pans under the table to reveal Gideon with only one leg.*)

Later in the scene, after Hannibal has sliced the meat and prepared a plate of food which he places in front of his guest,

> Dr. Gideon: You expect me to be my own last supper?

> Hannibal: Yes.

The brilliance of the program lies in the way the character Hannibal speaks into culture about greed, consumerism, narcissism, and mimetic rivalry that space does not allow us to go into. What we can say here, however, is

10. "To approve falsehood instead of truth so as to err in spite of himself, and not to be able to refrain from the works of lust because of the pain involved in breaking away from fleshly bonds: these do not belong to the nature of man as he was created before the fall. They are the penalty of man as now condemned by original sin." Augustine, *On Free Will*, 202.

11. Žižek, *Living in the End Times*, 73.

that the act of eating, the art of the meal, is elevated way beyond hunger satisfaction to the impact humanity has upon one another. The irony of the program is that we are not created to use and consume one another like the products we relentlessly buy; rather, we are created for relationship. How often have we sat around food and shared some of our most wonderful experiences? How often has the event of sharing food together provided some of our most profound moments in relationships with others? In the same way, sex is not simply an act to satisfy sexual hunger; rather, it is given as a gift to share in depth of relationship with another, to express a love shared between two people, an act of self-giving love. But it will never fully express the fullness of love, for only fullness of relationship with God is able to do that. This is a love that goes beyond sexuality and finds us at our divine desire, a desire that has its roots and purpose in God.

WHO ARE WE?

Paul makes the outstanding assertion in his letter to the Galatian churches that in Christ all religious-ethnic differentiation has been replaced with humanity now being incorporated into the Person of Jesus, baptized into his death, raised with him in his resurrection. No longer is humanity defined according to "Jew or Greek," "slave or free," "male and female," but all are now a new creation, a new-creational community whose identity is found and determined in and through Christ. Irenaeus saw creation on a journey, created good with the goal and orientation towards perfection. So even humanity, "male and female" created "very good" and for relationship with one another, were never seen to be the finished article, the goal in and of themselves; Jesus has always been humanity's goal. Sin, violence, and death led us away from this *telos*, disoriented us, and led us astray. Yet perfection was never found in the "male and female" and the distinctions we have; rather, it is found in Christ, the goal and perfection of humanity. Jesus, not Adam, is the goal of humanity. Whereas before Christ our relationships were determined by the Law, differentiations determined by social and ethnic distinctions, now, in Christ, our relationships are a sign of redemption, a glimpse of the redemptive power of God, a "new creation" where the old order of things has passed away. What this now means is that all relationships of non-violent, non-coercive love can be an expression of our ultimate relationship in Christ when one day God will be all in all. In other words, because humanity's goal is Jesus, as Paul clearly states, and because we are not defined by our "male and female," *any* relationship that reflects the unconditional love of God and enables us to glimpse at God's ultimate reconciliation is to be celebrated.

Gregory of Nyssa said, "It seems to me that what we hope for is nothing else than the Lord himself."[12] For Gregory, humanity would not be fully and truly created until "the unification of all mankind, joined in looking toward the same goal of their yearning"[13] with "the genuine life made manifest in us none other than Christ himself."[14] His sister Macrina held a similar line in which she asserted that the "goal towards which each single economy in the universe is moving" is none other than "the transcendent good of the universe,"[15] namely Christ. In other words,

> The creation itself will be set free from its bondage to decay and will obtain the freedom of the glory of the children of God. We know that the whole creation has been groaning in labor pains until now; and not only the creation, but we ourselves, who have the first fruits of the Spirit, groan inwardly while we wait for adoption, the redemption of our bodies. Rom 8:21–3

> He is the beginning, the firstborn from the dead, so that he might come to have first place in everything. For in him all the fullness of God was pleased to dwell, and through him God was pleased to reconcile to himself all things, whether on earth or in heaven, by making peace through the blood of his cross. Col 1:18b–20

Humanity is waiting, waiting to be made truly human by the True Human, waiting to be fully incorporated into his resurrection life, waiting for all things to be reconciled to himself. Sexual desire is, then, a glimpse at divine desire. For in our sexual desire we are expressing a longing for intimacy with God. Again, such language may seem difficult to grasp, but as discussed earlier, all desire, no matter how disoriented and destructive it is, springs from a desire within humanity for the "transcendent good of the universe." We are created to be in relationship with our Creator, so we search and scratch and seek to be incorporated into that Life, often with very little awareness that this is what we desire. In our sexual desire there

12. Gregory of Nyssa, *Homilies on the Beatitudes*, quoted in Pelikan, *Christianity and Classical Culture*, 323.

13. Gregory of Nyssa, *Commentary on the Song of Songs*, quoted in Pelikan, *Christianity and Classical Culture*, 312.

14. Ibid, 321.

15. Gregory of Nyssa, *On the Soul and the Resurrection*, quoted in Pelikan, *Christianity and Classical Culture*, 325.

is a waiting and a longing, and then in our erotic ecstasy, when humanity expresses itself sexually at its best, we discover something of the divine life breaking into the moment. We leave our solitude and our own space and invite another to join us there, sharing in "the loss of boundary of skin . . . to meet in a shared space, a shared breath."[16] At the reconciliation of all things, humanity will discover at last what it means to truly love God and love one another. We will be "sharers in the divine nature" (2 Pet 1:4) and have an intimacy with God that will go beyond all previous intimate and loving encounters. We will be fully known. Therefore,

> . . . sexual desire is . . . the "precious clue" woven into our created being reminding us of our rootedness in God, to bring this desire into *right* "alignment" with God's purposes, purified from sin and possessiveness . . .[17]

Sex is rightly seen then in light of the Trinitarian Life of Self-giving love, unshackled from selfishness and disoriented desire. Our calling is to seek that the Spirit might bring our desire into God's own desire. God loves his creation, and in God's yearning for us we encounter our own yearning. Sex is a reflection of God's continued outpouring love of himself to his creation, to humanity. Our yearning springs from the fact that God yearned for us first:

> We love because he first loved us. (1 John 4:19)

True love, a love that flows from God's own nature, will be expressed well through sexual desire and practice, and will enable us to discover our humanity, rehumanizing us from all the ways sex has been used to dehumanize us. Ultimate "human oneness with the *One*" will not happen through being bogged "down in human binaries which themselves resist the Spirit,"[18] but rather through the embrace of the Spirit's leading into self-giving, non-violent, non-coercive, grace-filled, unlimited, forgiving, loving relationships. Jesus Christ is the One we are called to imitate in all things, so we are each invited to share in the Oneness of relationship that the Trinity has. Jesus' prayer, "I in them and you in me, that they may become completely one . . . "[19] is the prayer for humanity, that in our identity we may know oneness with one another, united in love, redeemed in our relationships, reconciled in God.

---

16. Irigaray, "Questions to Emmanuel Lévinas: On the Divinity of Love," 111.

17. Coakley, *God, Sexuality and the Self,* 309–10.

18. Ibid, 331.

19. John 17:23a.

Conclusion

Waking Up

Having fully awakened from his dream, the dreamer—or former dreamer—might momentarily reflect upon the ingenious intricacy of the distortions by which his sleeping mind had transformed the world around him into another world altogether. . . . It is only because a dreamer has temporarily lost the desire to turn his eyes toward more distant horizons that he believes he inhabits a reality perfectly complete in itself, in need of no further explanation. He does not see that this secondary world rests upon no foundations, has no larger story, and persists as an apparent unity only as long as he has forgotten how to question its curious omissions and contradictions. . . . How remarkable that, when the critical intellect has fallen dormant, the imagination is still capable of such feats of invention . . . the reality of things was present all along, but only under the guise of another reality altogether. This is something, though, that one can appreciate only in the light of morning, once one has emerged from dreams. For, while those who have awakened know what it is to sleep, those who are still asleep do not remember what it is to be awake.[1]

Inception was a film all about dreams, and yet was in fact a film that challenged the viewer to question reality. What is real? What is merely a dream landscape that I am walking through? As Bentley Hart points out in the above quote, only those who are awake know what it is to sleep, yet those who are asleep are unaware of what it means to be awake. *Inception*

1. Bentley Hart, *The Experience of God*, 291–2.

leaves you wondering what it means to be awake and what it means to be asleep. Dream and reality blur together in the film, and we are often left wondering whose dream and whose reality we are inhabiting. What if we were seemingly endlessly asleep, captivated by our dreams, no longer able to differentiate between the real world and the dream world?

Throughout the film, Leonardo DiCaprio's character is seeking one goal, and that is to be reunited with his children. Each time we are introduced to his children, it is merely a flashback of them playing in the garden, their faces obscured. By the end of the film we are none the wiser as to whether he has been reunited or not, left to our own judgments and imagination as to the outcome. Is it the final realization of his "dream" to be reunited with his children, or is it simply a dream that he will replay forever to somehow ease yet also heighten his despair?

What *Inception* does so beautifully is to highlight the possibilities available to us in our dreams, creating new landscapes and endless possibilities according the level of our imagination. And this is what Bentley Hart paints so poetically in the quote above. All that we dreamed was part of a present reality, yet under a guise of another reality that only comes to light in the light of the day when we awake. And awake we must, for if we do not, we will continue in a despairing reality that will never be realized.

The ghost of perfection would have us walk endlessly in the landscape of dreams, captivated by our seemingly ingenious distortions of reality, yet all we have done is "lost the desire to turn [our] eyes toward more distant horizons," failing to see the reality beyond this ghost that is never quite present. But there is One who does meet with us, in often unexpected and surprising ways, stirring us from our fantasies and into a lived reality,

> Early in the morning he came walking toward them on the sea. But when the disciples saw him walking on the sea, they were terrified, saying, "It is a ghost!" And they cried out in fear. But immediately Jesus spoke to them and said, "Take heart, it is I; do not be afraid." Matt 14:25–7

In Jesus we encounter the True Human, and such a sight is often too much for us to take. We instinctively cry out in fear, believing that what we see is a ghost, a ghost of perfection. Yet Jesus speaks a better word than our cries of fear, a word of peace: "Do not be afraid." In his perfect love our fear is cast out. Our fear causes us to grasp and strive and desire to get hold of that which we think we have not got enough of, a perfection of humanity, a version of life that actually reflects our deepest fears. This is the ghost of perfection that we strive for and yet will never lay hold of, for it will always vanish from our grip the moment we seek to draw it closer to ourselves. We come to believe that God is about to do something we never imagined, perform the miraculous we have been striving and searching for. So we pray and fast and long and struggle for God to do something tomorrow. And we miss the Now, we miss Today:

> See, now is the acceptable time; see, now is the day of salvation!
> (2 Cor 6:2)

This ghost of perfection will never quite be in sight, always veiled behind empty promises, broken dreams, and faded, weary hearts. We find ourselves confused and scared, never sure where to turn or how to move forward, our very identity seemingly as hazy and elusive as the ghost we keep searching for. Yet there is One who meets us in the midst of our dreams and reality, draws us up from our terror, and gives strength to our hearts. Again and again Jesus speaks to us, "Take heart, it is I; do not be afraid."

In Jesus we initially believe we have seen another ghost of perfection, One who cannot possibly be anything like we imagined. Indeed, Jesus is not anything like we imagined—he is far better, far greater, far more beautiful and wonderful. Jesus is not the construct of a broken and wounded humanity who are trying to create something that will feed a utopian future. Rather, Jesus is True Humanity, revealing all that humanity is called to be and ultimately will be. The human imagination is not able to take in who God is and how he has revealed himself to us through Jesus.

> We are overwhelmed. God's inexhaustible creation, limitless grace, relentless mercy, enduring purpose, fathomless love: it is too much to contemplate, assimilate, understand. This is the language of abundance . . . a tidal wave of glory.[2]

So we construct a Jesus in our own image, a Jesus who is more like us, a Jesus who is more palpable to our ghost-hunting imaginations. And yet Jesus is not like us; rather, we are called to be like him in order that we might discover our true identity, an identity that is found "in Christ." So much of our angst and destructive behaviour results from our lack of knowing who we are, what our identity is, because we do not know who Jesus is.

God is the God of unending, limitless, unconditional love, mercy, grace and forgiveness. There is no limit to the forgiveness of God, no end to

---

2. Wells, *God's Companions*, 7.

his mercy, no amount of wrongdoing that can ever exhaust the forgiveness poured out in the person of Jesus.

God is the God of mercy, not sacrifice.

God does not require blood or sacrifice; he does not require violence in order to transform our humanity and the cosmos into a "new creation."[3] Rather, it is through the nonviolent, forgiveness-fueled redemptive purposes of God that all things will be made new, where "all will be well and all manner of all things will be well." There is no wrath in God, no violent contagion in him that needs to be overcome, no judgment he is waiting to deliver. Rather, it is our violence that needs to be overcome, our wrath that needs destroying, our judgment that needs dealing with. The measure we judge by is the measure of our judgment. The violence we sow we will reap. The wrath we deliver is what we will experience. Only in following the unlimited Way of forgiveness modeled by Jesus can our violent ways be overcome. Jesus alone is the One able to overcome our wrath, violence, and judgment. Indeed, at the Cross, he has overcome: "It is finished!"

So we wait, glimpsing at the Kingdom of God breaking into our own lives, at times flowing out of us like streams of living water bringing nourishment to those around us producing marvel within us as our fragile clay-like work is used by the Spirit of God to display His effervescent love.

Yet all too often we are drawn once again into our own dreamed fantasy, forgetting what humanity is through the lens of Jesus, and find ourselves groping for the ghost.

> While they were talking about this, Jesus himself stood among them and said to them, "Peace be with you." They were startled and terrified, and thought that they were seeing a ghost. He said to them, "Why are you frightened, and why do doubts arise in your hearts? Look at my hands and my feet; see that it is I myself. Touch me and see; for a ghost does not have flesh and bones as you see that I have." And when he had said this, he showed them his hands and his feet. While in their joy they were disbelieving and still wondering, he said to them, "Have you anything here to eat?" They gave him a piece of broiled fish, and he took it and ate in their presence. Luke 24:36–43

---

3. "Therefore, the Lord, recapitulating this day in himself, suffered his Passion on the day before Sabbath, that is to say, the sixth day of creation, that on which the human being was created, thereby offering to it a second creation through his Passion, the new creation free from death." Irenaeus, *Against Heresies*, 5.23.2.

When the Risen Jesus appears to us, we are "startled and terrified," for we cannot comprehend the True Human. We are so entangled in our sin and violence that when the Prince of Peace is before us in his forgiving grace-presence, we are truly afraid. Humanity throughout its history has imitated one another in our rage and violence, escalating in our aggression and retaliation until a suitable scapegoat can be found. Collectively we transfer our hostility upon the one whom we have blamed and judged in order to quell our fears and alleviate our violent passion. Our violence is imitated, something we each learn from the other, passing it on from person to person, learning it from culture to culture. We are not individual, independent, free, and autonomous beings; we are who we are through the relationship we have with others. As Michael Hardin points out,

> We have a long tradition of being ourselves as autonomous individuals, each responsible for ourselves, each making choices that define who we are. We have failed to recognize that this way of "being human" is a false construct. The reality is that we are all in this thing of humanness together; there is no such thing as "free will" if we are always copying each other non-consciously. . . . So many contemporary philosophical, political, and social problems could be solved if it were recognized that we are not really autonomous but interconnected as a species.[4]

The ghost of perfection is not flesh and bones, cannot be touched or even seen. The ghost of perfection does not invite us to eat together with it in its presence and does not bring joy and wonder to our lives. The ghost of perfection reveals our human violence, our imitative rivalistic desires that can only be transformed through the power of divine forgiveness. "Jesus' intention is to draw us out of the box of our pagan sacrificial logic, out of our idolatry, and into the wonderful mystery of his compassionate Abba."[5]

God is present with us by the gift of His Spirit, and so we know Jesus as Risen Lord; we have encountered the depth and breadth of the love of God in his presence and have come to recognize little by little who we are being made into the image and likeness of:

> Only in Jesus . . . did the image of God appear with full clarity.[6]

---

4. Hardin, *The Jesus Driven Life*, 154.

5. Ibid, 116.

6. Pannenberg, *Systematic Theology Volume II*, 216.

We are not who we were, because we are redeemed through the life, death, and resurrection of Jesus. But we are not yet who we will be as we are redeemed through the life, death and resurrection of Jesus. We are redeemed and restored in our relationship with the living God, invited into the Divine Dance of the Trinitarian Life, reconciled to God and one another; Jesus' "resurrection is the foundation of a totally new existence; peace, shalom, forgiveness."[7] In the presence of the Risen Christ something changes: "Peace be with you." To be human is to "See what love the Father has given us that we should be called children of God; and that is what we are. The reason the world does not know us is that it did not know him. Beloved, we are God's children now; what we will be has not yet been revealed. What we do know is this: when he is revealed, we will be like him, for we will see him as he is."[8]

The ghost of perfection strips us of our humanity, calling us to lives of fearful violent desire, never present, seen, or within our grasp, yet always urging us on in fractured, broken, and selfish ways. The Risen Jesus vanquishes the dark mist of this ghost and meets with us in His perfect love, waking us up, beckoning us by His Spirit into the Oneness of His Father's self-giving life. This is an invitation to discover humanity, an invitation to be like him, the rehumanizing of the dehumanized.

---

7. Hardin, *The Jesus Driven Life*, 153.

8. 1 John 3:1–2.

Bibliography

Antonello, Pierpaolo, and Gifford, Paul, eds. *How We Became Human: Mimetic Theory and the Science of Evolutionary Origins*. East Lansing: Michigan State University Press, 2015.

Athanasius, *On the Incarnation*. Translated by A Religious of C. S. M. V. London: Mowbray, 1953.

Augustine, *City of God*. Translated by H. Bettenson. New York: Penguin, 1997.

———. *Confessions*. Translated by R. S. Pinie-Coffin. Reading: Penguin Books, 1988.

———. *Earlier Writings*, Translated by J. S. Burleigh. Westminster: John Knox Press, 1953.

Bailey, Doug, et al., "Transhumanist Declaration." http://humanityplus.org/philosophy/transhumanist-declaration/

Barna, George, *Marketing the Church*. Ventura: Regel Books, 1990.

Barth, Karl, *Church Dogmatics*, vols. I–IV. Translated and edited by G.W. Bromiley and T.F. Torrance. Edinburgh: T & T Clark, 1956–75.

———. *God Here and Now*. London: Routledge, 2003

Bartholomew, Craig, and Moritz, Thorsten, eds. *Christ and Consumerism*. Carlisle: Paternoster Press, 2000.

Bauman, Zygmunt, *Consuming Life*. Cambridge: Polity Press, 2007.

———. "Living in Utopia." https://www.respekt.cz/respekt-in-english/living-in-utopia

Bentley Hart, David, *Atheist Delusions*. London: Yale University Press, 2009.

———. *The Doors of the Sea*. Cambridge: Eerdmans, 2005.

———. *The Experience of God*. London: Yale University Press, 2013.

———. *The Story of Christianity*. London: Quercus, 2009.

Bernasconi, Robert, and Critchley, Simon, eds. *Re-Reading Lévinas*. London: Athlone, 1991.

Bonhoeffer, Dietrich, *The Cost of Discipleship*. Minneapolis: Fortress, 2000.

———. *Ethics*. Minneapolis: Fortress, 2000.

———. *Life Together*. London: SCM Press, 1954.

———. *Meditations on the Psalms*. Grand Rapids: Zondervan, 2002.

Bosch, David, J., *Transforming Mission*. New York: Orbis Books, 1991.

Brewin, Kester, *After Magic*. London: Vaux, 2013.

Brueggemann, Walter, *The Prophetic Imagination*. Minneapolis: Fortress, 2001.

Calvin, John, *Institutes of the Christian Religion*. ed. J. T. McNeill, trans. F. L. Battles; Philadelphia, P: Westminster Press, 1960.

Chouraqui, André, "The Psalms" in *Cistercians of Strict Observance*, Vol. 29, Number 1 (1995) 3–31.

Clement, *The First Epistle of Clement*, in ANF, vol. 1, 5–21.

Coakley, Sarah, *God, Sexuality, and the Self*. Cambridge: University Press, 2013.

Colwell, John E., *Promise and Presence: An Exploration of Sacramental Theology*. Imprint Carlisle: Paternoster, 2005.

———. *Why Have You Forsaken Me?* Milton Keynes: Paternoster, 2010.

Connolly, John, *The Unquiet*. London: Hodder, 2007.

Dionysius, *The Works of Dionysius*, in ANF, vol. 6, 81–120.

Durham, John, I., *Exodus*, Word Biblical Commentary 3. Waco, TX: Word Books, 1987.

Ellul, Jacques, *Violence: Reflections from a Christian Perspective*. Oregon: Wipf and Stock, 2012.

Farrow, Douglas, "St Irenaeus of Lyons: The Church and the World," *Pro Ecclesia*, IV/3 (1995), pp. 333–55.

Florovsky, Georges, "Empire and Desert: Antinomies of Christian History," *Greek Orthodox Theological Review* III/2 (1957) 133–59.

Frost, Michael, Hirsch, Alan, *The Shaping of Things to Come: Innovation and Mission for the 21st Century Church*. Massachusetts: Hendrickson Publishers, 2003.

Girard, René, *Things Hidden Since the Foundation of the World*. London: Continuum, 2003.

Gregory of Nyssa, *The Life of Moses*, trans A. J. Malherbe and E. Ferguson. New York: HarperOne, 2006.

Gregory Nazianzus, *Epistle to Cledonius the Priest Against Apollinarius*, http://www.monachos.net/content/patristics/patristictexts/158.

Gunton, Colin. E., *The Promise of Trinitarian Theology*. Edinburgh: T&T Clark, 1997.

Hardin, Michael. *The Jesus Driven Life*. Lancaster: JDL Press, 2010.

———. *Reading the Bible with René Girard: Conversations with Steven E. Berry*. Lancaster: JDL Press, 2015.

Harris, Thomas, *Hannibal*. London: Arrow, 2000.

Hauerwas, Stanley, *Approaching the End*. Grand Rapids: Eerdmans, 2013.

———. *The Peaceable Kingdom* (London: Notra Dame Press, 1983)

Hauerwas, Stanley, Vanier, Jean, *Living Gently in a Violent World*. Illinois: IVP, 2008.

Hitchens, Christopher, *God is Not Great: How Religion Poisons Everything*. New York: Warner Twelve, 2007.

Irenaeus, *Against Heresies*, in ANF, vol 1, 315–567.

James, Oliver, *Affluenza*. London: Vermilion, 2007.

———. *The Selfish Capitalist: Origins of Affluenza*. London: Vermilion, 2008.

Jameson, Frederic, "Historicism in The Shining," in *Signatures of the Visible*. London: Routledge, 1992.

Jenson, Robert. W, *Systematic Theology*, vol. 2, *The Works of God*. Oxford: Oxford University Press, 1999.

John of the Cross, *A Spiritual Canticle of the Soul and the Bridegroom of Christ*. London: CreateSpace Independent Publishing, 2015.

John of Damascus, *Exposition of the Orthodox Faith*. Buffalo, NY: Chrsitian Literature Publishing, 2012.

Justin Martyr, *First Apology*, in ANF, vol 1, 159–302.

Kierkegaard, Søren, *Fear and Trembling*. Reading: Penguin, 2005.

King Jr., Martin Luther, "Nonviolence and Racial Justice." *Christian Century*, (1957) 118–22.

King, Stephen, *The Green Mile*. New York: Pocket Books, 1996.

Lacan, Jacques, *Écrits: A Selection*. New York: Routledge, 2001.

———. *The Seminar of Jacques Lacan XI*. New York: W. W. Norton & Company, 1998.

Lederer, Florence, *The Secret Rose Garden of Sa'd Ud Din Mahmud Shabistari*. Grand Rapids: Evinity Publishing Inc., 2009.

Long, Michael, ed. *Christian Peace and Nonviolence: A Documentary History*. New York: Orbis Books, 2011.

Lossky, Vladimir, *In the Image and Likeness of God*. St Vladimir's Seminary Press, 1974.

Lunn, Nigel, *The Original Ending of Mark: A New Case for the Authenticity of Mark 16:9–20*. Eugene, OR: Wipf and Stock, 2014.

Luther, Martin, *Luther's Works: Word and Sacrament I* vol. 35, eds. Helmut Lehmann and Theodore E. Bachman. Philadelphia: Fortress Press, 1960.

MacIntyre, Alasdair, *Marxism and Christianity*. London: Duckworth, 1995.

Masson, Jeffrey, M., *The Assault on Truth*. London: Ballantine Books, 2003.

Maximus the Confessor, *Ambiguum 7* [Eng. translation], ed. Andrew Louth. New York: Routledge, 1996.

McGee, Margaret, D., *Haiku, The Sacred Art: A Spiritual Practice in Three Lines*. Vermont: Sky Light Paths Publishing, 2009.

McGrath, Alister, E., *Historical Theology: An Introduction to the History of Christian Thought*. Oxford: Blackwell, 1998.

Niebuhr, Richard, H., *Christ and Culture*. San Francisco: Harper and Row, 1975.

Nietzsche, Friedrich, *Thus Spake Zarathustra*. London: Bibliophile Books, 1997.

Oswald, Andrew, J., "Afflenza: A Review." http://www2.warwick.ac.uk/fac/soc/economics/staff/academic/oswald/affluenzajan07.pdf.

Pannenberg, Wolfhart, *Systematic Theology Volume II*. Translated G. W. Bromiley. Edinburgh: T&T Clark, 1994.

Pelikan, Jaroslav., *Christianity and Classical Culture*. London: Yale University Press, 1993.

Pelikan, Jaroslav, ed. *Luther's Works*, vol. 35, *Word and Sacrament*, "Preface to the Psalter." 254. Philadelphia: Fortress, 1960.

Peterson, Eugene, *The Message*. Colorado: Naypress, 2002.

Pound, Marcus, *Theology, Psychoanalysis and Trauma*. London: SCM Press, 2007.

Rollins, Peter, *The Divine Magician*. New York: Howard Books, 2015.

Schwager, Raymond, S. J., *Must there be Scapegoats?: Violence and Redemption in the Bible*. New York: The Crossroad Publishing Company, 1987.

Stasiuk, Andrzej, *The Cardboard Aeroplane*. Wydawnictwo Czarne: Wolowiec, 2000.

Stoker, Bram, *Dracula*. London: Wordsworth Classics, 2000.

Tertullian, *On Idolatry* in ANF, vol 3, 61–78.

Thomas Aquinas, *Summa Theologica*. Translated by Fathers of the English Dominican Province. Westminster, MD: Christian Classics, 1981.

Tillich, Paul, *The Essential Tillich*. New York: Collier Books, 1987.

Weaver, Denny, J., *The Nonviolent Atonement*. Grand Rapids: Eerdmans, 2001.

Webb, Lance, *Conquering the Seven Deadly Sins*. Nashville: Abingdon Press, 1955.

Wells, Samuel, *God's Companions: Christian Ethics and the Abundance of God*. Oxford: Blackwell, 2006.

Williams, Rowan, "Angels at Peckham Rye" http://www.churchtimes.co.uk/articles/2007/16-march/faith/angels-at-peckham-rye

———ˇ *Silence and Honey Cakes*. Oxford: Medio Media, 2004.

Wink, Walter, *Engaging the Powers*. Minneapolis: Fortress Press, 1992.

———. *The Powers that Be: Theology for a New Millennium* (London: Cassell, 1998)

Witherington III, Ben, *The Acts of the Apostles: A Socio-Rhetorical Commentary*. Carlisle: Paternoster Press, 1998.

Wolterstorff, Nicholas, *Lament for a Son*. Grand Rapids: Eerdmans, 1987.

Žižek, Slavoj, *Enjoy Your Sympton!:Jacques Lacan in Hollywood and Out*. New York: Routledge, 2008.

———. *God in Pain: Inversions of Apocalypse*. New York: Seven Stories Press, 2012.

———. *Living in the End Times*. London, Verso, 2010.

———. *Looking Awry: An Introduction to Jacques Lacan Through Popular Culture*. London: The MIT Press, 1992.

———. "A Perverts Guide to Family." http://www.lacan.com/zizfamily.htm

———. *Puppet and the Dwarf: The Perverse Core of Christianity*. London: The MIT Press, 2003.

9 781532 614897